A. E Small

A Treatise on the Decline of Manhood

Its Causes, and the Best Means of Preventing their Effects, and...

A. E Small

A Treatise on the Decline of Manhood
Its Causes, and the Best Means of Preventing their Effects, and...

ISBN/EAN: 9783337091125

Printed in Europe, USA, Canada, Australia, Japan

Cover: Foto ©Thomas Meinert / pixelio.de

More available books at **www.hansebooks.com**

A TREATISE

ON THE

DECLINE OF MANHOOD;

ITS CAUSES,

AND

THE BEST MEANS OF PREVENTING THEIR EFFECTS, AND
BRINGING ABOUT A RESTORATION
TO HEALTH.

BY

A. E. SMALL, A.M., M.D.,

PRESIDENT OF HAHNEMANN COLLEGE AND HOSPITAL, ETC.

THIRD EDITION—REVISED AND ENLARGED.

—

CHICAGO:
DUNCAN BROTHERS.
1885.

PREFACE TO THE THIRD EDITION.

In preparing this edition for the press, the entire text has been thoroughly and carefully revised, and new matter has been added. It is hoped that the work, as revised, will merit a continuance of the favorable recognition extended to the previous editions by the profession.

PREFACE TO FIRST EDITION.

In furnishing the following treatise on the "CAUSES THAT INDUCE THE PREMATURE DECLINE OF MANHOOD," and the most judicious means of removing them and curing their effects, the author is aware of the many difficulties in the way of producing anything like a satisfactory treatise upon the subject. But from many years' experience he has collected the results of his observations into the following pages.

The remedies employed have been such as he has found most effectual, and yet he is aware that in the hands of many practitioners other remedies have been employed not mentioned in this treatise.

The work is not arranged so methodically as the author could have wished, and yet his object will be accomplished if he has made any suggestions or thrown any light upon the subject that will aid the profession or redound to the benefit of the unfortunate.

With the hope, therefore, that this attempt to supply a want in the literature of Homœopathy will be charitably received, and pave the way for better efforts, the work is given to the profession and public.

THE AUTHOR.

CONTENTS.

		Page.
INTRODUCTION.	- - - - - -	9

CHAPTER I.

A General View of the Subject. - - - 11

CHAPTER II.

Spermatorrhœa from Inflammation and Irritation of the
Urethra. - - - - - - 17

CHAPTER III.

Masturbation. - - - - - - 22

CHAPTER IV.

How to Correct the Habit of Self-abuse and Cure its
Effects. - - - - - - - 34

CHAPTER V.

Continuation of the Effects of Self-abuse, Nocturnal
Emissions. - - - - - - 39

CHAPTER VI.

Sexual Excesses and Other Causes of Spermatorrhœa. - 45

CHAPTER VII.

Spermatorrhœa Caused by Ascarides and Gravel. - - 51

CHAPTER VIII.

Excessive Sexual Intercourse in Married Life. - - 59

8 CONTENTS.

CHAPTER IX.

The Consequences of Abnormal Seminal Emissions. - 64

CHAPTER X.

Consequences of Spermatorrhœa Affecting the Whole
System. - - - - - - - 76

CHAPTER XI.

The Effects of Spermatorrhœa upon the Respiratory
System and the Heart and other Organs. - - - 82

CHAPTER XII.

Marriage in Relation to Sexual Weakness. - - - 89

CHAPTER XIII.

Recapitulation and Treatment of Sexual Weaknesses. - 94

CHAPTER XIV.

The Application of Electricity in the Treatment of
Seminal Weakness. - - - - - 101

CHAPTER XV.

Clinical Directions. - - - - - 105

INTRODUCTION.

The chief object to be accomplished in writing a treatise on the causes that produce a premature decline of manhood, is to point out, explicitly, the best protection against them, as well as the most commendable measures of relief from their effects.

2. Sexual debility results from a variety of causes, which, in many instances, are avoidable, while in some instances it may be constitutional and dependent upon a general deterioration of the nutritive and nervous systems.

3. When the cause is known, the first inquiry is, can it be removed? and can the effect produced be remedied? No one suffers from the malady with indifference, and therefore, it may be concluded that every victim to sexual disorder desires radical relief.

4. From the nature of the affection, those who suffer are prone to seek aid from any source that promises it, and without some information of a specific nature that will lead to a proper discrimination, a resort

to nostrums and quackery, injurious in their results, too frequently happens.

5. As there are no two constitutions alike, and seldom that two cases of suffering are so precisely alike, that the same treatment will suffice for each, it is proposed to point out the several grades of the disorder in connection with the causes and treatment of each, when medical treatment is required. The kind of debility particularly under consideration in the following pages is generally known under the head of " Involuntary emissions of semen," which operates disastrously upon the vital condition of manhood.

CHAPTER I.

One of the main characteristics of sexual debility is frequent involuntary emissions of the seminal fluid, followed by a feeling of exhaustion. For strong, healthy and plethoric persons these emissions may occur occasionally without exciting undue apprehension of the result. But even in such persons, where the occurence is frequent and copious, great weakness and lassitude is apt to follow, betokening an abnormal condition, that requires both hygienic and medical treatment.

2. In those of vigorous manhood, and of superabundent vitality, the involuntary evacuation of the seminal vessels at times may be considered a conservator of health, and demanded for its protection. This is true so long as such persons remain conscious of their occurrence, unaccompanied by general malaise and lassitude.

3. Lascivious dreams are simply reflex symptoms conveyed from the distended seminal vesicles through

the nerves of the brain; and the most salutary remedy for emissions arising from this cause is through matrimonial alliance and the legitimate exercise of the function.

4. But emissions that occur without the cognizance of the patient, and without erections and pleasurable sensations, are of a different character, and may result from an abnormal irritability of the sexual organs, and if not arrested, they will deteriorate the general health and produce a gradual decline of virility.

5. The causes that operate to produce increased irritability are various, and merit separate consideration in order to arrive at the means of obviating them, and the most rational application of remedies to overcome the debility and promote strength. Some of these causes are avoidable, and require but a strong effort of the will to set them aside; others are unavoidable, being diseased conditions of the urinary organs, from which the increased irritability of the sexual organs proceeds. These causes can only be removed by well-chosen remedies, or by the skill of the operative surgeon.

6. From either class of causes excessive emissions may occur, differing only from normal seminal emissions in being involuntary and debilitating. The

seminal vesicles, ducts, and their orifices may severally participate in the irritability, and become so debilitated that seminal discharges are found to occur frequently, and on the slightest provocation. The simple act of urination, the effect at stool, or immediately after both, or when brought into proximity with female society, severally operate to provoke seminal emissions or consciousness of the loss. This is properly termed " spermatorrhœa."

7. Pathologically considered, these seminal evacuations arise from a variety of causes, and not, as is frequently asserted, from sexual excesses and abuses. They often result from other and quite different causes.

8. When seminal emissions arise from causes inherent in the system, their origin is so wrapped in obscurity that the real cause is overlooked, and, consequently, they are found to be the most persistent and difficult of cure. It is only when the true pathology of the disorder is discovered that we can arrive at a knowledge of the starting-point, so as to institute a rational or successful treatment. Anything short of this necessarily subjects the patient to continual drain upon his constitution and life. For without duly referring the symptoms to the veritable source from whence they proceed, so as to base a proper and curative treatment,

in spite of remedies given in accordance with symptoms alone the difficulty will progress until the health is undermined and the virility destroyed.

9. The matter must be probed to the bottom, or otherwise the symptoms are meaningless, and afford but an empty display of phenomena, as likely to mislead in the treatment as to favor its utility; for as a variety of causes, differing widely in their nature, may produce like effect, genuine skill, in the treatment of spermatorrhœa, must depend upon a knowledge of the real cause as a starting point.

10. A glance at the anatomy of the genito-urinary apparatus and its relation to neighboring parts, will convince any rational practitioner of the reasonableness of this assertion; for who can deny the fact that hard impacted fæces, pressing upon the seminal vesicles, operates to produce more or less disorder in the sexual organs? Who does not know that a mismanaged gonorrhœa produces the most disastrous consequences upon the testes? And why? Because of their intimate anatomical connexion.

11. Therefore, let us look after the various causes of seminal weakness, which, as so many fountains, send forth abnormal excitement to the genital organs, producing emissions and spermatorrhœa.

1. Urethritis from different sources. 2. Stricture of the urethra. 3. Affections of the rectum and anus. 4. Constipation, retained fæces. 5. Hæmorrhoids and varices or fissures. 6. Intestinal worms. 7. Chronic inflammation and tenesmus of the bladder. 8. Stone or gravel. 9. Spinal irritation. 10. Sexual excesses. 11. Masturbation. 12. Prostatitis. 13. Morbid imagination.

A careful examination of each of the above will enable us to rationally comprehend the relation between cause and effect in each particular case, and show us the total insufficiency of a merely symptomatic treatment of these diseases.

12. Either one or all of these causes have a close relation to the genital organs, and a continual irritation from either forms a source of determination of blood, congestion, swelling, excessive irritability of the testes, spermatic cord, seminal vesicles, prostate gland, and veru-montanum, and thence erections at first, and seminal emissions. In time the erections cease; the membrum-virile becomes flaccid, and the fluid constantly passes off, altered in quality, thin, and void of the characteristic spermatozoa. With this general view of the subject we may form some idea of

the nature and extent of the malady under consideration.

Note.—Before entering on the consideration of the various causes of spermatorrhœa, the author wishes to impress on the mind of mothers and nurses the importance of looking critically after the interest of young children committed to their care. The nocturnal enuresis of young children, or " wetting the bed" as it is termed, denotes a chronic irritation of the bladder and urethra which, by *criminal neglect*, may engender the habit of self-pollution. This weakness produces such an irritation of the urinary passage as will give rise to early erections, so annoying to the child, that he pulls and rubs his privates until the lamentable habit of self-abuse is unconsciously acquired. Therefore it is criminal to neglect this primary condition of young boys, which so frequently leads to self-abuse. It is not sufficient to call it a bad habit and that the boy will out-grow it. All possible care and means must be called into requisition to effect an early cure. (See letter of Dr. T. C. Duncan, at the end of Chapter XIV.)

Intestinal worms in children, and especially ascari-des or pin worms, often prove to be an early proximate cause of self-abuse. The itching of the anus or private parts may induce a rubbing, pulling or scratching that unawares leads to the habit. In older subjects, gravel or tenesmus of the bladder may lead to the habit.

CHAPTER II.

Chronic inflammation of the urethra, from whatever cause, extends itself by means of continuity of structure not only to the bladder, uterus and kidneys, but also to the organs of reproduction. This inflammation may be produced, 1st, By mechanical injury, inflicted by instruments used by onanists, such as pencils or quills, which they introduce into the urethra to excite pollutions, when, from frequent and long continued abuse, the urethra becomes insensible to other excitants. Fragments of such instruments have been known to remain, forming a nucleus for inflammation.

Blows, bruises and other occasional injuries may provoke spermatorrhœa. The great sensitiveness of the urethra, and the unavoidable admixture of the urine with the blood, from such injuries, renders wounds or mechanical abrasions or squeezes of the greatest importance.

For from such sources chronic urethretis is liable to result.

To cure a spermatorrhœa, originating from causes of this kind, the unnatural use of the instruments must be banished; all pressure must be removed, and all positions leading to contusion or pressure upon the organ should be avoided, and then let moderately cold water be freely used for ablutions twice or thrice during the day. Arnica at first is an excellent remedy for internal administration, and drop doses may be taken several times daily until the soreness and irritability of the parts disappear; when the cause is removed the effect ceases. Should Arnica prove insufficient, injections of tepid water, with a few drops of the tincture of Calendula, may suffice. The distilled extract of Hamamelis may be used for the same purpose. When spermatorrhœa is dependent on this cause, Apocynum, Eupatorium and Senecio aurens 3.

2. Certain drinks and articles of diet produce an unfavorable action upon the urethra, and sometimes cause inflammation. Certain medicines, taken in excess, have the same influence, such as diuretics. The irritation produced by some liquors, such as gin, are proximate causes of involuntary seminal emissions. When oysters, crabs, or other shell-fish exert an in-

jurious action of the kind, refrain from using them. The same advice is given with reference to articles of food or drink or medicine known to exert an unfavorable effect upon the genital organs, and the spermatorrhœa that remains as an effect can be easily cured by well-known remedies.

A young clerk in a silk house suffered from involuntary emission several times a week, until the effect upon his health began to be noted. He applied to a physician, who inquired critically into his habits, all of which he found quite regular, excepting eating late at night. On inquiry it was found that he indulged freely in such food as eggs and oysters. He was advised to confine himself to regular meals, and to avoid both the eggs and oysters—to partake of beef, mutton, and vegetables, and avoid poultry and stimulating soups. At first but little change was noted; his digestion seemed somewhat impaired. Nux vom. 3d was given half an hour after each meal, and he soon recovered from the emissions and gained robust health.

Another young man, who suffered much from this difficulty, was constantly annoyed by difficult digestion and depressed spirits, was cured by Pulsatilla, 3; dose three times a day, after duly regulating his diet.

2. Another source of inflammation of the urethra is

infection from impure sexual exposure and in urethral stricture from chancre; from these an irritation is set up which results in pollutions of a serious character. To cure these, if they result from simple urethritis or gonorrhœa, and particularly if there is much smarting when urinating, Aconite may be taken first, and afterwards Cannabis sativa. Several cases of this kind have been noted: A gentleman of middle age having contracted gonorrhœa, which he supposed himself entirely cured of, was afterwards the victim of nocturnal emissions, which weakened his whole system. He was greatly depressed, and suffered inveterate constipation.

When constipation, proctitis or hæmorrhoids are proximate causes of spermatorrhœa the remedies suitable for these affections may be called into requisition with good effect.

He had applied to one physician after another without benefit, until he despaired of finding relief. He finally consulted a Homœopathic physician, who minutely inquired into his antecedents, and then prescribed Nux vom. to remove the constipation; after Nux, Lycopodium was given, and his bowels moved freely, without difficulty. The 6th attenuation of these remedies was used. A diet of toast and steak in the morning, with a cup of black tea; beef or mutton with vegetables for dinner, and brown bread or toast for tea, was directed, Cannabis sativa 6th was given every six hours, for a week, in connection with this diet, and the patient found himself greatly relieved; and this treatment was afterward continued until he was completely rid of the difficulty.

Other cases were cured by addressing remedies directly to the proximate cause, and afterwards to the resulting symptoms. When the urethral irritation is subdued, and the pollutions still continue, Cannabis sativa or Cantharis will generally cure.

When stricture of the urethra is ascertained to be the existing cause of emissions, the stricture must be removed before the difficulty can cease. Sulphur 3d will often accomplish the whole, in connection with a well regulated diet. To secure regularity of the bowels, Nux v., Sulphur and Mercurius sol. may be used advantageously. Other remedies—Atropine, Bromide of Camphor, Hydrastis, Bromide of Iron.

As one of the most effective remedies for spermatorrhœa, we may name electricity when properly used by an experienced electrician, when the administration of remedies indicated by the symptoms fails of effecting a cure, this resort has been effectual. (See Chap. XIV.)

CHAPTER III.

MASTURBATION.

We shall now consider a cause of urethral irritation which by many is believed to be one of the most deteriorating vices incident to the youth of both sexes. Very early in life boys have been initiated into habits of self-abuse, and if no one finds an opportunity to advise and counsel them otherwise, by pointing out the dangerous consequences of the practice, the habit becomes fixed and difficult to break. After a while such a youth begins to grow sickly, pale, nervous, and unmanly, and unless the habit is arrested in time, and the victims become sensible of the danger, his approach to manhood is fraught with entailed consequences, that finally render him an object of pity and disgust. Youth of fifteen or sixteen summers, who indulge in this vice, may soon bring about an irritation of the urethra that merges into real inflammation, attended by a secretion which has a close relation to pollutions and spermatorrhœa. It is our purpose, therefore, to treat this subject somewhat in detail, in order to give an insight into the best remedial measures for the protection of virility.

2. Immediately before the age of puberty and during the transition period, as well as after, unknown longings and desires assert their supremacy in the youthful mind. These are the first utterings of sexual instinct, though scarcely recognized as such by the subjects. Some arrive at this period earlier and some later. In peculiarly irritable constitutions the instinct after puberty manifests itself with great intensity, and exhibits its effects in certain tendencies to bodily ailments and frailties.

3. When by the allurements of others such youth are initiated into solitary habits of exciting the genitals, first by filling the mind with impure thoughts and imaginings, and then by manual interference, the most pernicious and degrading habit of self-pollution steals over them, and soon results in physical weaknesses which are prophetic of the early decline of manhood.

4. The defect of early education, coupled with direct temptation and the allurements of evil association, often form the basis or starting-point for a career of miserable habits, that sooner or later prey upon the

mental and physical constitution. When once initiated and predisposed, both mind and body become subject to excitement from otherwise trivial causes. Novel reading, love stories and sickly sentimentalism of every kind, become disastrous allurements to the habit of masturbation. These allurements and dangers often override the rigid supervision of parents and educators, and beset the youthful and impressible mind in many different ways.

It is a fact no less sad than true, that very many in their tender years, and even in childhood, are brought through one means or another into mental excitement and thence into actual abuse of the genital organs, which becomes a habit of greater or less injury.

By such abuses the genital organs become impaired and diseased, and the strength and life of the entire organism becomes undermined.

These excesses are so extremely dangerous and inevitably ruinous to body and mind that it is of the utmost importance to detect and arrest them before it is too late, and to promote this end young boys should be subject to the kindest and most friendly supervision, and every prudent effort should be made directly and indirectly to withdraw them from such influences and habits as excite sexual phantasies, and without acquainting them with the friendly object intended, great care should be exercised in diverting their minds from all misleading thoughts and inclinations before they have become so rooted that all attempts to obliterate them prove a failure.

To accomplish this, requires:

1. A provision of suitable and useful employment for mind and body.

2. To withhold all kinds of seductive reading and theatricals, and all imprudent mixing with the opposite sex, such as allowing them after early childhood to occupy the same sleeping apartments and to share the same couch. Experience and observation have established beyond a doubt the imprudence, if not the wickedness, of allowing such practice.

3. But at suitable times and under the supervision of proper restraints, boys and girls should be encouraged in outdoor sports and open air exercise. It is a mistaken idea to suppose that the cause of virtue is promoted by keeping them secluded from the society of each other. For such is not the case. The reverse often begets that sickly, unhealthy secret brooding that creates a want of self-respect and dread of social intercourse. It is far better that boys should have the advantage of associating in suitable plays and

pastimes with girls of their own age, while at the same time, every moral and elevating influence should be exercised over them by their parents and guardians.

4. If a suspicion exists that boys indulge in self-abuse, let them be quietly watched until the truth is ascertained. An inclination to be alone and in secluded places often excites suspicion of self-abuse, and especially if after such seclusions they seem pale and excited, or depressed and morose, or peevish and fretful. And unusually timid boys and young men addicted to self-abuse are generally shy and timid. They betray an absence of manhood and appear cowardly; and moreover, the countenance betrays with nearly the same certainty as it does the tippler or opium eater, and when interested and affectionate friends learn from these signs the painful fact, their friendly aid is demanded, they should point out to the erring youth the sad effects that must inevitably follow this habit. Many a boy, bright and lively at ten years of age, has become dull, sickly and mentally dejected before his twenty summers by such miserable self-abuse. A slow, hesitating speech, a blundering mode of speaking, a bad memory, and dullness of apprehension in general, are the usual fruits of this sin; and since so much is at stake, and the guilty ones are

so prone to deny their pernicious habits, no prudent means of detection should be neglected. If necessary, the bed linen and shirts should be called into requisition to afford confirmation of the fact, and if caught in the practice, let them be told in a fartherly and affectionate way the disastrous consequences, not once only, but many, many times, until the habit is subdued.

5. This course will hardly fail to make a favorable impression on young and pliable minds, and if the will power at first is inadequate, gentle encouragement and the aid of solicitious parents will greatly stimulate resolution till the habit is conquered.

When made fully sensible of the dreadful consequences of self-abuse, there are but few so reckless and incorrigible as to countenance and continue the habit. Mechanical means of restraint has sometimes been found necessary to aid the efforts of young men in dissipating the inclination and practice. The best medical counsel may also be necessary to aid in bringing about this desirable result, and it would be adding crime to crime to withhold any measure capable of arresting the criminal practice.

We have thus far treated of masturbation as a crime involving the voluntary surrender of manhood. But now we propose to consider other causes that may induce the habit, that places the victim more in the light of a sufferer than in that of a sinner. Ascarides or pin worms in the rectum sometimes induce an itching that implicates in no small degree the genitals of young boys, and compels them to scratch and rub until they unconsciously fall into the habit of masturbation. Herpetic eruptions that burn and itch may compel similar habits, terminating in the same way. The reason why the habit operates so injuriously upon the entire organism, whether induced by vicious allurements, morbid broodings, or sickly love stories, or by diseased conditions as detailed above, is because of the close proximity and relation of the sexual apparatus to the spinal cord, thence to the brain, which first receives the shock and then by reflex action the urinary and digestive systems become affected. But the injury does not stop here, the mind becomes filled with impure images exciting the brain, and thence the memory and mental faculties. It finally ends in hypochondria, melancholy and suicide, or in epilepsy, apoplexy or dementia.

The intensity of the shock which the habit imparts, to the whole system, and the consequent prostration and debility must especially prove injurious to the organs properly supplied with nerves. The stomach, therefore, is liable to become distended, and nutrition is seriously interrupted; the entire body as a consequence fails of receiving sufficient nourishment, it gradually gets weaker, the nerves become unstrung and disposed to paralytic weakness and cramps; and as during the act, there is a determination of blood to the brain, frequent cases of apoplexy have terminated the fatal habit; or otherwise 10 or 15 per cent. of the number of inmates of the lunatic asylums prove to have been the victims of this vice.

Self-abuse has another peculiar effect, if not early arrested; it destroys sexual enjoyment and entails coldness in the conjugal bed, and begets disappointment and unhappiness and completely frustrates the fulfillment of marriage relations.

It is to be feared that many who attain to a marriageable age refrain from entering into wedlock by reason of the cold indifference toward the institution, which results from this vice. They prefer the mistaken enjoyment of solitary self-abuse to the satisfaction of legitimate sexual intercourse.

It will be seen, then, that self-abuse requires greater exertion of the sexual organs than a natural embrace, and that they are weakened by oft-repeated and un-

natural irritation, as the opportunities are more frequent than for natural intercourse, and the constrained
position of standing or sitting must prove more injurious to muscles and nerves that are brought into
requisition, it follows conclusively that greater muscular and nervous weakness must result from the act.
It is also manifest that in a natural embrace the excitement is participated in by two, whereas in self-
abuse it is entirely cultivated by one's own imagination, and must therefore prove the more exhausting.
Self-abuse is more dangerous because it withdraws its
victims from society and leads to solitary dwelling
upon themselves, or to musings and broodings of so
low a quality that they fall into the pit of melancholy
and thus make complete shipwreck of health and life.

In order to place safeguards around unsophisticated
youth and boys in early life, parents and teachers must
be vigilant and ready to comprehend the importance
of directing their thoughts and habits in the right direction at first.   They should teach them to avoid such
plays as suggest and often prove the beginning of injurious habits.   It is far better to avoid the causes of
urethritis at first than to be successful even in curing
pollutions and spermatorrhœa.

As boyhood and youth passes away, and manhood

supervenes, strictures produced by indiscretions of youth, may be the constant cause of spermatorrhœa. These strictures arise from various causes; the worst and most difficult to cure are for the most part traced to badly treated gonorrhœa. But those arising from the cicatrices of wounds, or from urethral chancre, are caused from the folding of the mucus lining of the canal, and are sufficiently formidable. For the folding and swelling and formation of valves by fibrous indurations of the mucous membrane, are tedious in duration and difficult to cure. Strictures generally have their seat in that portion of the urethra where the inflammation has been the greatest and the suppuration the most apparent. There may be more than one near or more remote from the orifice of the bladder. The narrower and longer they are the greater the obstruction to the passage of urine and semen, and the portion posterior to the strictures becomes distended, and presses indirectly upon the seminal vesicles so violently as to weaken and injure, and thus be the source of an obstructed spermatorrhœa.

Strictures may also produce other obstructions more and more interiorly until effete and irritating matters which should be thrown off meet with obstructions, and are thrown back upon the delicate seminal vesi-

cles, and result in weakening them to a degree that
destroys their normal functions, or so paralyzes the
tenacity of the ducts as to allow the seminal fluid to
flow off unnoticed without any sensation or erection ;
in this way spermatorrhœa results, and impotence becomes inevitable.

The effects of masturbation not only extend to the
urethra, prostate gland and bladder, but to contiguous
structures. The rectum becomes affected—the sphinc-
ter-ani contracts, varices and hæmorrhoids are severally the result of urethral irritation. Stricture and
frequent urging to urinate, hæmorrhages from the
bowels, prolapsus and all the various hæmorrhoidal
ailments sometimes refer themselves to the same cause,
though too frequently overlooked, and on this account
a misdirected treatment is liable.

Spasmodic strictures as well as those caused by urethral inflammation, may result from self-abuse, and
also those resulting from enlarged veins of the urethra,
from gouty deposits, urinary calculi, and forcible cath-
eterization, may provoke spermatorrhœa or emissions.

Since strictures are so often the cause of seminal
weakness, and self-abuse may be the first cause of the
urethral inflammation that produces them, it is well
to be familiar with the symptoms of stricture that

they may receive early attention. The first symptom is the retarded flow of urine, and also the urging to force the urine by reason of some sensible obstruction, behind which the urine accumulates; the stream is changed in form and volume, at first very small, afterward sluggish, and finally a mere dribble from the urethral orifice. This departure from the normal standard is marked that no one can fail to discover it.

Spinal irritation is often the cause of much disturbance and weakness of the seminal vesicles, but masturbation constantly persisted in may cause spinal irritation. But if from a mechanical injury or a cold, there results a spinal irritation. Seminal weakness may occur as a consequence.

CHAPTER IV.

HOW TO CORRECT THE HABIT OF SELF-ABUSE AND CURE ITS EFFECTS.

1. It is for parents and guardians to impress extremely young subjects with the wickedness and danger of the practice, to watch over them and correct them for every known indulgence. There is but little difficulty in correcting this abuse while the victims are very young and before the habit is confirmed.

2. When boys are associated together and become each other's instructors in the vice, let such associations be broken up. Older boys often initiate younger ones and fill their susceptible and tender minds with lewd thoughts, and great care to guard against evil associations is absolutely requisite when such, before the age of puberty, begin to exhibit that peculiar cast of the countenance and debility consequent upon such early vice. Let them be impressed that the debility and sickness is brought on by the crime. Strengthen the

impression by holding up the terrible and almost fatal results that will surely follow, if they habitually repeat the act or allow themselves to be misled by wicked associates. When first debilitated, give such, in connection with moral restraint, Cinchona 6th dilution, ten drops in half a tumbler of water, and give a desert spoonful three times a day. The above is the proper treatment when the self-abuse has been wickedly initiated by older delinquents.

3. Parents should so carefully guard the health of their children as to obviate all diseased conditions liable to induce scratching or rubbing the genitals, for in this way the habit of masturbation may be acquired; pinworms or seat worms of the anus produce a disastrous itching, and so do herpetic eruptions in the vicinity of the genitals, and too great care cannot be exercised in determining whether or not such disease exists. If the fact becomes established; for the pinworms, give Sulphur 6th, ten drops in half a tumbler of water, dessert spoonful every night; if this does not allay the itching, follow with Nux vomica in the same way, and teach the boy not to scratch or rub. If there is any eruption that causes much itching of the parts, Sulphur taken as above is required. In scrofulous children these troubles are liable to occur and be the

means of spontaneously initiating them into the habit of self-abuse; cure the cause, and with proper instruction the effect will cease. Ammonia 6th, Calcarea carb. 6th, and sometimes Petroleum 6th, with suitable moral restraint, will prove sufficient to correct these abuses.

4. To cure self-abuse in boys after they have passed the age of puberty, requires in part the same measures as for those younger. They must be impressed with the heinousness of the crime, if voluntarily committed; and also with the inevitable consequences upon the physical and mental health. Nothing can cure them or break them but a determined resolution to renounce the habit. To aid them in doing it, suitable employment for mind and body must be provided; and they must be made to realize that the practice is a sin against God. No protection against the vice is certain but a voluntary refraining from it from the highest of all motives; that it is a sin against God and an abuse of themselves.

5. To correct these morbid states of mind that favor the habits, let the youth be supplied with entertaining and useful reading, and if already there is more or less disturbance of the organic functions, which react upon the brooding and susceptible mind, remedial measures are necessary.

6. To guard against the disposition to self-abuse, Calcarea carb. 3d trituration, may be given every evening for a week. If there is any disturbance of the digestive system follow the Cal. c. with Nux vomica 3d, every evening one hour before retiri g for another week, observing at the same time to engage in such amusements as chess and other intellectual games, and sometimes in dancing or base ball. If the onanist finds himself weak, let him take China 3d. If he has stiffness of the back or some pain in the small of the back, let him take Cocculus 3d. If after the habit is subdued any debility remains, China 3d, may be taken three times a day until the debility is overcome. When the genitals are easily excited and suggest a return of the habit, Phos. ac. 3d, in water will be found useful. Morbid erections and lascivious dreams require Cantharis 3d, three times a day.

7. We have thus pointed out the ways that generally lead to self-abuse, as well as the surest means of arresting the habit, and it may be remarked that onanism once fixed is classed among the most inveterate of habits. But it can be cured if proper attention is bestowed to the right kind of discipline and medication. The longer the habit remains the more deteriorating the effects upon the nervous system, and

thence upon the nutritive functions. For the acute effects which arise from excessive rather than from long continued abuse we have named as remedies, China, Cocculus and Phos. ac., to which may be added Merc. sol. 3d, and Selenium. But for slow chronic effects, Sulphur may be given at long intervals, or perhaps, Carbo vegetabilis, and a generous diet.

For weakness and flaccidity of the penis, China may be taken three or four times a week.

For excessive nervousness and timidity, Calc., Phos. ac. may be taken in daily doses.

If there is a dull, indefinable bewilderment and sub-acute headache, Nux vomica, or perhaps, Zincum met. will often cure.

For the minor consequences that remain after the habit has ceased, the above remedies are of the greatest importance.

CHAPTER V.

By these emissions are understood seminal discharges that occur during sleep, and are dependent upon an enfeebled condition of the seminal vesicles, and irritation as the predisposing cause, that for the most part result from previous self-abuse. They differ from spermatorrhœa in taking place from excitement of the genital organs and erections, which seem to be produced by lascivious dreams, or by reason of the bladder being filled with urine. The quality of these discharges does not differ materially from the normal character of healthy semen; nevertheless they result from debility that has been induced from some cause of irritation of the urethra or weakening of the seminal ducts.

2. Those which are entailed as an effect of masturbation first demand our attention, because they occur frequently and sometimes nightly, and are followed by

great weakness and depression. The victims of these emissions often are made unhappy and wretched, because they know that habits which they have succeeded in conquering were the primary cause, and they often seem willing to endure the suffering than to apply for relief. But disease from any cause may be curable, and such is the case with regard to these nocturnal emissions. We have had considerable experience in the treatment of such cases, and undoubtedly they are generally curable.

3. In the case of a young man who had been guilty of self-abuse until seventeen years, on being aroused to his condition he voluntarily abandoned the habit, and turned his attention to a conscientious religious life. But his whole system was greatly impaired. He was dyspeptic and nervous, depressed and melancholic, and found himself the victim of almost nightly emissions. He sought a confidential medical adviser, who at once comprehended the nature of his suffering. For more than a year he had refrained from the polluting habit, hoping that his health and strength would return to him without obliging him to resort to a physician. But on the contrary, he found his health declining he fancied himself the victim of imbecility, and his mind was filled with fearful forebodings of a disastrous future.

4. The first measure of relief resorted to by his physician was to encourage his hopes and direct his mind from himself to the consideration of topics that would be most likely to give a healthy tone to his moral and religious aspirations. He further taught him that the study of arithmetic and the solution of its problems upon slate or blackboard would strengthen his manly faculties, whereas the reading of sentimental stories would have the opposite effect. All of which, the young man seemed to appreciate.

5. After pointing out a mental and moral course that would favor a radical cure, the physician commenced with him a course of medical treatment. Finding his patient the victim of excessive sexual excitement, he first gave him the sixth decimal attenuation of Cantharis, four globules three times a day, and prohibited the use of all stimulating drinks, including coffee and all stimulating aliments calculated to excite sexual feelings, such as oysters, crabs, lobsters, etc. The first prescription was continued for five or six days, and the young man felt a sensible relief. But feeling dull and stupid, having a dread of society, and still suffering, but less frequently, from emissions, Phosphoric acid 6th was given in water three times a day; there was a gradual improvement, and the emis-

sions were less frequent. The patient, as directed, confined himself to a light nutritious diet, under which his strength improved; occasional seasons of malaise and weakness were cured by China 3d. For two years his whole system became more and more robust, and he rejoiced in finding himself radically cured.

6. For the debility brought on by onanism, China is quite generally the best remedy, and it only requires an early cessation of the habit, a careful diet, and a good occupation for the mind, as well as a persistent perseverance with this remedy to effect a perfect restoration to health.

7. For emissions brought on exclusively by this vice, attended with extreme sense of weakness, provided a proper attention is paid to diet and employment for the mind, China will seldom fail of curing. Aurum muriaticum will often cure when given daily in the 3d centesimal trituration.

8. For the depression of spirits and nervous restlessness, Hypophosphite of Lime in the 3d trituration, taken in three-grain doses morning and evening, will suffice. But the remedy must be taken a sufficient length of time to ensure its effect.

9. Nightly emissions have been cured by Digitalis in

those of bilious temperament subject to melancholy. The 3d dilution is employed, but for any treatment to be successful the cause must be removed. The diet should be well regulated, the mind must be accustomed to dwell upon profitable subjects, and there must be a firm reliance upon the remedies. In addition to those already cited for nocturnal emissions, Sepia often has a salutary effect, and in some inveterate cases Sulphur 3d, taken in daily doses, will effect a radical cure.

10. A student of theology, aged twenty-five, found his health declining on account of the debilitating effects of nocturnal emissions, which were brought on by self-abuse in early life. He applied for medical treatment. The 3d aqueous dilution of Phosphoric acid, while under a strict regimen as to diet, was administered three times a day for a month; after which his health improved rapidly, and he rejoiced in finding himself no longer troubled with the emissions. He was enabled to pursue his studies without difficulty.

11. A young man desirous of entering into matrimony, hesitated on account of the state of health which early self-abuse had entailed. He suffered from frequent involuntary emissions when asleep, and from the consequent loss of mental vigor and physical strength which usually follow. Alarmed on this ac-

count, he sought advice and medical treatment. He complained of a dull pain in the region of the lumbar vertebræ, and flaccidity of the penis. He suffered from tedious constipation and hæmorrhoids, that often protruded from the anus; Nux v., 3d trituration, was first prescribed—a three-grain powder every night half an hour before retiring—after which he was somewhat relieved of constipation; but there was no improvement in other respects. Sulphur 6th was then substituted for the Nux v. and continued for a week; no good result followed; Conium mac. 6th dilution, ten drops in a tumbler of water, was directed to be given in tablespoonful doses, morning and evening. He soon felt better, and after two weeks the hæmorrhoids disappeared, the pain in the back was better, and normal virility returned. A short time after the young man got married, and has lived happily with his wife for the last five years, and is the father of two children, a son and a daughter.

12. Conium 3d, 6th and 30th attenuation have been advantageously employed in the treatment of nocturnal emissions, or those that occur involuntarily at other times, when there is a flaccidity of the membrum virile and a sense of weakness and pain in the back.

CHAPTER. VI.

SEXUAL EXCESSES AND OTHER CAUSES OF SPERMATORRHŒA.

By spermatorrhœa is understood the unconscious loss of the seminal fluid when at stool or when urinating, or at other times from the most trivial exciting cause, when there are no erections, but a mere flaccid state of the penis. The first cause of this weakening discharge which we shall consider at some length, is SEXUAL EXCESSES, *both in unmarried and married life.* In the former a reckless roaming lust, and the frequenting of brothels, wherewith to become satiated by frequent indulgence, are the primary causes of genital weakness that result in the premature decline of manhood. The effect of excesses of this kind, for the sake of gratifying the mere lust for variety, is to bring upon the victim a train of evil consequences hardly to be enumerated. First, upon the vital condition of the general organism; and second, upon those organs essential to the integrity of manhood. After a general

debauch, there is a complete derangement of the functions, nutrition becomes impaired, and the entire body
suffers; and this is not all, the mind participates in
the general wreck and the victim bocomes polluted in
soul and body throughout. Frequent repetition soon
reduces the victim to the lowest point of physical and
moral degradation. At first his digestion is impaired,
and he resorts to a stimulating diet to encourage his
lusts; then follows constipation, hæmorrhoids and
other ailments that, in conjunction with a corrupt
longing for sexual pleasures, so deteriorate and weak-
en the sexual system as to destroy all power of re-
taining the seminal fluid, and it passes off in spermatorrhœa as readily as feculent matter passes from the
bowels in chronic diarrhœa. The state of his mind is
even worse than that of his body; sickened by his own
indulgence he at last hates the opposite sex, and never
conceives of it the idea of chastity. Such is the effect
of commencing a career of indulgence of roaming lust,
irrespective of the consequences. Is there no remedy
for a reckless youth of this description till all is lost?
Before the habit is confirmed by repeated indulgence,
it is possible to break off such a career and voluntarily
refrain and reform, but as the habit becomes more and
more confirmed by illicit intercourse with a variety of

courtezans, there is the greatest danger of the complete wreck of manhood. Who is able to utter a successful warning before it is to late to save the victim from becoming a mere driveler and a show, with genital weaknesses that inevitably lead to absolute destruction of virility, and, a confirmed spermatorrhœa?

2. The most inveterate of all maladies to cure are those found in such a wreck of humanity—the fruits of unconquered lust. Nevertheless, so long as a spark of humanity remains, or in other words, so long as any moral sense remains, a struggle to reform is possible. When a manly struggle is made to break off lewd practices, and the mind is withdrawn from lewd imaginings, there is at least some hope of recuperation and recovery from the effects of debauchery. If the digestion is impaired and the stomach irritable, and rejects the food taken into it, Pulsatilla 6th, in doses of four globules, three times a day, may be taken when there is a sense of weight in the stomach or a sense of contraction. Nux vomica 6th may be substituted for the Pulsatilla.

3. After Pulsatilla and Nux have done their work, China 6th may be taken in the same way. In case of constipation and accumulation of hardened feculent matter in the rectum, Lycopodium 6th may be taken

morning and evening in connection with a diet of digestible meats and vegetables, with bran bread, fruit such as aples and pears, and no stimulating condiments. Great regularity in taking the meals, and the repudiation of late suppers, oysters, etc., are essentially necessary. Agnus castus is a remedy not to be overlooked.

4. In case of hæmorrhoids that become inflamed and effect contiguous tissues so as to produce or augment spermatorrhœa, Æsculus glabra tincture may be taken in drop doses in a spoonful of water, and repeated every three hours. In very many cases this remedy will remove the piles, and if the spermatorrhœa remains and the seminal fluid passes off when urinating or straining at stool, Selenium 3d, or Conium 3d may be dropped in the proportion of ten drops to half a goblet of water, and a tablespoonful dose may be taken every four hours during the day. A strict observance of the above course will accomplish much in recovering the lost manhood.

5. For varices or tumid veins that become so sore and painful as indirectly to produce weakness, if not paralysis of the seminal vesicles, Arnica and Pulsatilla are remedies to be consulted.

6. Affections of the rectum and anus that have resulted from other causes than sexual excesses, may

produce spermatorrhœa, and before the latter can be cured these affections must be removed, and well chosen remedies for the particular troubles often have a salutary effect.

7. Retained fæces, by pressing upon the seminal vesicles, induce a semi-paralytic state of the muscular coat, disabling them so that they cannot resist the pressure of the fæcal masses when at stool, and the seminal fluid passes off involuntarily. Similar effects may occur during the act of urinating by the contraction of the bladder. In every case, therefore, of spermatorrhœa, the state of the bowels and the condition of the urinary organs should be critically looked after, and such remedies must be selected as will be most likely to remove the proximate cause, and in a majority of cases Nux vomica or Lycopodium will suffice; a dose of either every night may produce relief.

8. Fissures of the anus, which are accompanied by cramplike contractions of the sphincter ani, and pain at stool, tend to retard the evacuations and cause retention of fæces. The itching and tickling of these are of great importance in explaining many cases of spermatorrhœa. The intolerable itching compels scratching the perineum and anal region; the adjacent tests suffer from daily irritation provoked by this act. The organs contiguous participate in the irritation,

and this is often followed by weakness and spermatorrhœa, without sexual excitement. Sulphur, the 3d
trituration, taken in three-grain doses, every night,
will generally cure the fissures and remove the itching, and consequently effect a cure.

9. Herpes, which consists of numerous minute vesicles upon the scrotum, penis or perineum, and around
the anus, may burn, itch and smart, and provoke the
patient to rub and scratch until the genitals become
so weakened that spermatorrhœa may be occasioned.
To remove this condition, Petroleum has been found a
specific.

10. A gentleman of steady, temperate and virtuous
habits, was almost maddened by this herpetic eruption, and spent much time and money in striving for
relief, was at last advised to take Petroleum, the 3d
attenuation, five drops in a spoonful of water, night
and morning, and in less than two weeks he was
entirely cured.

11. When the seminal vesicles are no longer able
to serve as reservoirs for the seminal fluid by reason
of the constant irritation which produces depression
and weakness, and on the slightest provocation discharge their contents, there results an habitual spermatorrhœa. Petroleum as above may be given first,
and afterward Sulphur to cure the difficulty.

CHAPTER VII.

The effect of thread worms upon the sexual sphere is both dangerous as well as distressing. They generate in the large intestine, and to this circumstance must be attributed the importance of some persons who, through their annoying influence, have been initiated into self-abuse, and thence into suffering from seminal losses and spermatorrhœa. Very young boys often become the victims of suffering from these parasites, and comparatively a less number of adults find themselves victimized by their presence.

2. This inconsiderable worm is cylindrical and pointed, white in color, about the size of common wrapping twine used for tying up small parcels. The tail end of the male ends abruptly, and is rolled up in a spiral, while in the female, it is straight and pointed.

3. The head is provided with wing-like attachments, between which the mouth is situated; the length varies from a line to a line and a half. It sometimes

appears in the evacuation in large numbers, so great
even as to present the appearance of a constant wrig-
ling motion.

4. When we consider the great number of symptoms this worm is capable of producing, such as tickling the nose, squinting, colic, fits, etc., it is not difficult to comprehend the nature of its action upon the
anus in producing that intolerable itching which is so
hard to endure, and not only the anus, but the intes-
tines, testicles and penis, and the most sensitive seminal vesicles, exciting them to involuntary, emissions
by self-abuse, or to pollution and spermatorrhœa.

5. Thread worms produce nearly the same symptoms
as stone in the bladder; children two or three years
old suffer constant erections from them. This symptom affords one of the most positive indications of the
presence of pin worms, and these boys grow up with
the constant habit of handling the parts that itch, and
scratching and rubbing habitually comes up with them
in some form of self-abuse.

6. The opposite sex likewise suffer in the same way,
and are led into habits of self-abuse, until health dis-
appears, and beauty fades. This constant itching and
scratching irritates the skin, causes the clitoris to be
reddened and swollen, and sometimes an ichorous dis-

charge from the vagina, and this only augments the itching, burning and swelling of the labia, all of which are powerful influences in augmenting self-abuse. We shall discuss this matter more fully when we enter upon the chapter relating to females entirely.

7. A learned authority, in treating of this particular affection and its consequences, gives as an indication of the presence of pin worms, deeply-sunken eyes, surrounded by blue rings. This appearance persists as an outstanding sign of self-pollution, even after the habit has been subdued and only its consequences remain; and what are the consequences that remain after the habit has been corrected? We will see if we can divine.

8. Hypochondriasis, impotence, congestion of the brain, apoplectic fits, may all occur from the irritation produced by these apparently insignificant vermin, though all indulgence in self-abuse is done away with, and moreover all these affections have been cured when the worms have been removed. Whenever a boy or girl is found to be suffering from epileptic fits, inquire critically into their habits, and whether they have been sacrificed to the ascaris. Should it be ascertained that pin worms were preying upon them, correct self-abuse, destroy the worms, and nine times

out of ten the epilepsy will prove to have been mere epileptiform convulsions caused by these iniquitous thread worms, and the patients will speedily recover.

9. A celebrated writer mentions a case of frequent nocturnal emissions of six years standing, which recovered rapidly after the removal of the pin worms, which it seems had been the cause. For all other means had previously failed, and the rapid convalescence of the patient after their destruction, proves them to have been the cause. This case, continues the writer, was also characterized by apoplectic symptoms and a partial loss of memory.

10. This writer is of the opinion that young men who are suffering from diurnal emissions, without erections or pleasurable sensations, were victims of enuresis during their childhood. In such cases the disease consists in great irritability and weakness of the bladder, increased by the warmth of the bed, and conducted from the bladder to the neighboring sexual apparatus.

11. The neck of the bladder is the most sensitive when stones are trying to make their exit, and from this source the most intensely painful symptoms proceed. The more the disease we call "gravel" is prolonged, the longer the durations of those affections of

the bladder, and so much more extensive is the inva-
sion of the contiguous parts or organs—the ureters,
kidneys, prostate gland, urethra, rectum and vagina,
all become implicated and somewhat exposed to danger.

12. The peculiar pains at the neck of the bladder,
as well as at the base, while walking, sitting at stool,
etc., and especially the pains experienced at the end of
the urethra, induce the patient to violent pulling and
stretching of the penis, and this leads to masturbation.
Excessive length of penis, and an observable lengthen-
ing of the prepuce, as well as a thickening of the
same, indicate the presence of stone in the bladder.

13. Sudden interruption of the flow of urine takes
place when small stones are carried into the urethra
and remain there. The reflex action of this irritation
upon the rectum, vagina, testicles, kidneys, etc., as
shown by cramp-like contractions of the perineum,
may produce an abnormal irritation of the whole urinary and genital apparatus. The tickling which stones
in the bladder produce in the membrum virile often
provoke involuntary emissions, and by the irritation
being transferred to the seminal vesicles, testicles and
seminal ducts, frequent pollutions and spermatorrhœa
results, and so far as the physical health is concerned,
these may as well be brought on by masturbation.

14. A single large stone in the bladder, firmly imbedded in the fundus, may by its weight alone exert so strong a pressure upon the seminal vesicles that they must empty their contents and gradually suffer a diminution from atrophy, to the detriment and destruction of the generative function. In this way no other cause than stone in the bladder may be the cause of spermatorrhœa and impotence.

15. The treatment of spermatorrhœa from these causes consists in removing them. For that caused by thread worms, such remedies must be employed as will exterminate them. Sulphur is an important remedy to give first—a dose of the 3d trituration may be given every day for a week. This remedy may be followed by Santonin 2d trituration, in the same way. Should these not be sufficient, Terebinth, in drop doses may be given twice a day, and other remedies, Calc. Cina and Ignatia. A timely use of these remedies will in a majority of cases effect a cure.

16. To cure the spermatorrhœa that has been provoked by stones in the bladder, requires great care. The cause must be removed, or otherwise there is no chance for a cure; when the stones are so large that they cannot pass through the urethra while urinating, and so hard and compact as to preclude the possibility

of their reduction by any other process, the sooner some skillful surgeon performs the operation of crushing them the better. It is preferable to undergo the pain of lithotomy than to struggle a long time in such suffering. After the operation has been successfully performed, the after treatment with remedies must be in accordance with the symptoms. The soreness and pain consequent upon the operation is very soon relieved by Arnica 6th, ten drops in half a tumbler of water, and a tablespoonful may be taken three times a day. Urging to urinate or painful urination requires Cantharis to be prepared and taken the same as Arnica. Urethral inflammation calls for Cannabis sat. It may be that these remedies will cure the seminal weakness after the cause has been removed. But if they fail, it must be attributed to the extensive injury which the seminal vesicles have already received. The perisstent use of China may in time bring up their vitality.

17. A young gentlemen who had always lived a correct life, was somewhat rheumatic. He observed that his urine deposited a reddish sediment, which stuck fast and adhered to the vessel. In process of time he passed what he termed red sand when he urinated. He finally began to suffer from strangury and irritation of the urethra. At last he felt stinging when he

urinated that extended to the end of the penis. Now, in our opinion, if this young man had taken at that· time a few doses of Tart. emetic, he might have had less suffering in the future. But he neglected himself and the difficulty grew worse, until he began to pass blood with his urine, and the heat and irritation was communicated to the testes and seminal vesicles exciting pollution and spermatorrhœa. The concretions in the bladder became so massive that lithotomy was a thing indispensable, and a skillful surgeon placed him in position to operate, put him under the influence of Ether, and effectually crushed the deposits, so that they readily passed off with the urine, after which he took Arnica and Cannabis and felt quite relieved, but the pollutions remained and frequently the semen would pass off with the urine, and when at stool. Digitalis given in drop doses of the 3d dilution had a good effect. Hypophosphite of Lime was given three times a day for a week or ten days, and the patient had no trouble afterward.

18. The diet in the cases should be barley water for drink, fruits, esculents, and good digestible meat and fish; all food tending to bind up the bowels so as to render constipation habitual, must be avoided.

CHAPTER VIII.

Marriage is intended for a higher, holier and happier purpose than unlimited indulgence in sexual intercourse. It is not a license for excessive coitus, and therefore when made such the worst of consequences may follow. First, weakness of the general system; second, weakness and derangement of the function of reproduction.

1. Weakness of the general system is produced by a series of disturbances which we will proceed to explain. When a man and wife cohabit for the sake of the legitimate purpose of begetting offspring, there is but little tax upon the strength or but little risk of impairing the generative function. But when the mind sinks into the low plane that craves sensual sexual indulgence, it morbidly and selfishly anticipates the most unlimited sway for the passions, and to gratify them is liable to become the chief motive and delight. Now there is a normal delight in sexual intercourse alto-

gether different from the morbid craving for indulgence. The former is chaste and pure when it spontaneously occurs from mutual love and affection between married partners, and virility is constantly
strengthened for the purpose; with such the love looks
to the important result—the legitimate fruits of marriage, and rejoices when children are born as the mutual
pledge of connubial affection. But the latter is a mere
sensual lust that looks no higher than for opportunities to gratify it. It despises the idea of rearing a
family, and the children that chance to be born as the
consequence of this indulgence are not welcomed as
blessings, but as necessary evils.

2. There is a limit to this morbid and selfish lust.
The gratification of it does not strengthen connubial
tenderness and affection, nor promote the health of
the parties. After a time the love grows cold, or is
turned into hatred, and frequent and continual indulgence ends in the deterioration of mind and body.

3. The man from continual losses of semen finds his
digestion impaired, his nervous system weak, and what
is worse he finds himself the victim of sexual weakness
and his virility impaired. His wife at the same time
has become hysterical and fretful, and there is no happiness in the household. The man and the woman only

come together when lust excites them to an embrace. At other times their backs are turned to each other in disgust and hatred.

4. Continual cohabitation at length destroys the function of the seminal vesicles, and paralyzes the little muscles that prevent the escape of the seminal fluid, and thus manhood becomes sterile, prostrated and the victim of spermatorrhœa, and the woman has become his sterile companion. Excessive sexual indulgence has been the proximate cause. When the digestion has become impaired, and the successive chain of organic functions participate in the misfortune, nutrition becomes feeble, and the whole body suffers from emaciation and debility. The effect upon the woman is quite similar. She suffers from nausea, debility, and general nervous prostration. The picture is not over-wrought. Excessive sexual indulgence, even in married life, results in the premature decline of manhood. It pollutes the soul and fills the mind with diverse fancies—it destroys the vital elasticity of the muscles, saps the nervous system and entails many weaknesses, such as rheumatism, constipation, hæmorrhoids and renal disturbances.

5. When all the vital functions become thus impaired from over-indulgence in sexual intercourse, the

query arises, Is there no remedy? Is the restoration
of strength possible, and can manhood be restored?
If not too low or too far gone we answer these ques-
tions affirmatively.

6. When one sensibly feels that his virility is wanting, let him pause and consider, let him direct his
mind and thoughts to a higher plane of love and affection, let him refrain from indulgence and lust and
turn his back upon the wicked practice. If he feels
feverish and restless, let him take a few doses of Aconite.
If his appetite is impaired and his food distresses him,
let him take Nux vomica. If his back is weak, rheumatic and stiff, let him take Cocculus. If his bladder
and urethra are irritated, let him take Cannabis; or if
he has strangury, let him take Cantharis; and for
general weakness, flaccidity of the penis and spermatorrhœa, let him take China persistently, and eat
and drink—if his appetite permits, and nutrition is
not completely interrupted—well cooked meats and
vegetables and drinks—wholesome drinks. If he ful-
fills these conditions without relapsing into more selfish indulgence of his passions, virility may be restored.

7. The worn out and depressed wife must also direct
her mind in that channel most conducive to her happiness. Let her thoughts and affections ascend and

rest in a religious view of married life. If she suffers from nausea and indigestion, she may improve the condition of her stomach by taking 3 grs. of the 3d trituration of Oxalate of Cerium. This remedy will strengthen her nerves, improve the digestion, allay the nausea, and give general tone to body and mind.

8. When both parties have thus complied with the means of regaining health and strength, they will be able to come together as man and wife, and with lofty sentiments above venery they will happily find connubial love and affection to take the place of lust, and they may come into the happy relationship of husband and wife. If otherwise, they will sink lower and lower, the victims of excessive lustful indulgence. Connubial bliss and conjugal tenderness will bloom no more for the household.

CHAPTER IX.

THE CONSEQUENCES OF ABNORMAL SEMINAL EMISSIONS.

Seminal emissions are either abnormal on account of the means by which they are brought about, or in respect to the frequency of their occurrence, whether produced by coitus or spontaneous pollutions at short intervals.

2. Long-continued and oft-repeated masturbation in both sexes is altogether abnormal, and is the fruitful source of disease. In the male it results in disease of the reproductive organs, and is followed by emaciation and consequent debility of the whole body. Hippocrates maintained that emaciation indicated the atrophy of the spinal cord. He describes the sense of formication, or the feeling, as if ants were crawling over the skin, as an accompaniment to the atrophy, and the loss of seminal fluid while urinating and when at stool as the result, and to this is added a sense of weariness and shortness of breath after a short walk. All this may occur when a person of the most robust health is broken down by the vice.

3. Celsus supports the views of Hippocrates, and maintains that atrophy of the spinal cord is the immediate source of emaciation and the legitimate consequence of abnormal emissions, produced by masturbation. It has been observed that the emaciation of onanists increases in spite of a good appetite, and the consumption of a large amount of food. Insatiable hunger and a good digestion are symptoms that indicate the struggle of nature to compensate for the losses, and yet so long as the spinal centre is the source and its atrophy stands out in continual decrease of the flesh, satiated hunger and an unimpaired digestion can avail but little. This emaciation is often ascribed to the rapid growth of youth that sometimes follows puberty. The muscles of the hip and lower extremities show forth this peculiarity, which is ascribed to pathological changes of the spinal cord.

4. Just in proportion to the emaciation the onanist loses his strength. He leaves his bed with difficulty in the morning, and is dull and listless during the day, even when at his work. In going up stairs he finds difficulty in breathing and palpitation of the heart. These symptoms of weakness may increase to an alarming extent, till the onanist bends over like an old man

and faints and reels from vertigo on the slightest exertion, and is obliged to keep his bed.

5. The case of the onanist even in the extremity described above, is not hopeless. The strength and fullness of the body may return when the vice is given up, and proper remedial means are employed to obviate the deterioration of the spinal cord. The habit broken, the appetite and digestion good, render it probable that the 3d decimal trituration of the Hypophosphite of Lime, given persistently for a sufficient length of time, will restore the spinal cord to its normal size and strength. The remedy may be administered in three grain doses, half an hour after each meal, and before retiring.

6. Modern physicians concur with Hippocrates and Celsus in these descriptions of the consequences of seminal losses by onanism. Hoffman says: "The onanist loses his strength after frequent seminal evacuations, the body gets thin, the face pale, the memory blunted or lost, and a continual coldness seizes the limbs; the face becomes idiotic, the voice hoarse, and in short, the whole body is reduced to atrophy, and sleeplessness, restlessness and tormenting dreams are the usual concomitant symptoms." The same author says: "Amaurosis or total blindness

is sometimes the consequence of abnormal seminal evacuations."

7. Boerhaave has noticed " pain in the membranes of the brain, weakness of the body, blunting of the senses, leanness and paralysis, and this is not all. The face loses its healthy and beautiful tint, becomes pale, earthlike ánd yellowish, or lead colored and livid; the lips pale and the eyes dim and glassy. The bluish margin around the eyes, a puffiness of the lids, flabbiness of the flesh, weak and small pulse, copious sweats, swelling of the upper and lower extremities, and finally hectic fever and general symptoms of exhaustion are the deplorable consequences which show that the organism does not succumb to the onslaught on its integrity without the most obstinate struggle." To change this condition requires, as before stated, a complete cessation of the polluting habit, and a steadfast resolution to rely on the best regimen and remedial means to restore the body to its normal health.

8. At first the abuse of the genital organs begets in the onanist a sense of hunger and a voracious appetite, but long continued sexual abuse results in indigestion, loss of appetite and disgust for food, or at best the appetite becomes irregular, vague and beset with morbid cravings and derangement of the sense of taste.

Food taken into the stomach causes pain and vomiting, or diarrhœa and flatulence or constipation and hæmorrhoids. For this condition Sulphur and Nux vomica may be given as follows: Upon the supposition that the victim is alarmed at the consequences and has broken off the habit which induces abnormal seminal losses, give Sulpher 3d, every night for a week, and then follow with a dose of the 3d of Nux v. every night just before retiring, and with such a diet as will accord with the condition of the stomach, the above consequences in many cases may be obviated.

9. Abnormal seminal emissions are said by Deslandes to lead to other diseases, classed among the severer and fatal forms, such as apoplexy, ramollissement, epilepsy, chorea, mental disorders, spinal irritation, blindness, deafness, gout, strabismus, varicocele, sarcocele and hydrocele, many of which are incurable, and they must therefore remain as a permanent warning to young men not to make shipwreck of themselves upon the rock upon which so many have foundered and sunk.

10. Another consequence of onanism is the complete decline of virility and inability to propagate their kind, either because they are unable to perform the marital act or because they have lost all the warmth

which healthy semen requires to vivify the female germs. Could such enervated individuals beget children, upon the principle that " like begets like," they will be feeble and puny, and as they grow to maturity they will be ill-shaped, bow-legged, oldish-looking specimens of humanity, and victims for an early grave. The more healthy, strong and sound the father, the more robust and perfect will be his offspring.

11. Bodily diseases alone are quite enough to utter a warning to the onanist. But they are trifling when compared with the awful consequences upon the soul. The mind succumbs, childishness and imbecility are its attributes, and he becomes a moral monstrosity; thank heaven, monsters cannot propagate, neither physical or moral, for manhood is gone, virility destroyed, and the vessel is a complete wreck in the sea of human infirmities. Such are the consequences of this kind of abnormal seminal losses.

12. As stated in the preceding chapter, a high, licentious degree of sexual abuse results in hopeless degeneracy of the organs of reproduction, as well as of the whole animal system. Their excitability gradually diminishes, and mental disorders, associated with their diseased condition, become prominent. This is especially the case when the body is well nourished with

good food, while at the same time the debilitating cause
continues to act on the genital organs. Pangs of conscience, remorse, shame or fear of the terrible consequences, as set forth in certain books, easily excite apprehension, melancholy and hypochondria. When the
mind constantly fights against the disease-producing
lust, it is in a continual state of excitement. The
brain becomes affected, and mental disturbance or insanity is superinduced upon the physical weakness, and
in the lust it changes to hopeless idiocy.

13. The conviction of incurable impotence, joined to
intemperate habits resorted to for the purpose of
silencing anxiety and fearful forebodings, frequently
contributes to unsettle the mind and pave the way to
hopeless dementia. One-tenth of all the inmates of
our insane asylums are of this class of secret sinners,
who still continue the vile habit of self-abuse, though
brought to spiritual and moral bankruptcy. Insanity,
hallucinations, loss of sight and hearing in a moral
point of view form the climax, characteristic of the
consequences, and withal these idiotic victims of sexual
abuse embrace every secret opportunity to instinctively
cultivate and practice the vile habit of onanism.

14. The consequences of masturbation in the female
sex are equally disastrous and injurious to the general

organism. Some eminent physicians maintain that the delicate and susceptible organization of the female system renders it more liable to suffer from this vice than that of the male. Suffice it to say the female masturbater suffers all the physical and mental deterioration that the practice induces in the opposite sex, and besides she becomes the victim of uterine affections of a serious nature, such as disturbance of the menses, prolapsus, displacement, ulcers, indurations and cancer.

15. One of the most serious consequences of the habit is local irritation of the nerves of the womb, resulting in nymphomania, which affects both soul and body, and degrades the finest feelings and attributes of her being—disgusting to herself, and a shock upon female or womanly modesty.

16. Rozier, a French physician, asserts that masturbation in girls, by the frequent and powerful cramp-like contractions accompanying the fulfillment of the act, induces considerable swelling of the neck, as in epileptics; and further, that in some the skin becomes yellow, and in others eruptions resembling ringworms make their appearance on the arms and legs, which disappear when thay refrain from the vice, but return when a repitition is indulged in. The voice, also,

of such girls becomes rough and hoarse, hollow and weak, losing its sonorous, soft and metallic ring.

17. A feeling of oppression in the chest and region of the stomach, with a dragging, occasionally indicating the need of food, are consequent on the habit. Severe cramps in the stomach, and similar disturbances of the solar plexus especially, show themselves in girls who indulge in this habit, and at the same time, leucorrhœa becomes established, attended with other troubles, such as spasms and cramps in various parts of the body, eructations after eating, distention of the abdomen, difficult digestion, headache and restless moving of the limbs.

18. A sallow countenance and an ugly expression of the face, which is pale and sickly, are signs which betoken the physical and mental depression, consequent upon masturbation. The vivacious expression of youth gives way, the eye becomes dim and surrounded by leaden colored rings, the lips are pale, the teeth covered with a gummy and dirty-looking mucus. The entire fullness of feminine spirit and beauty has seemingly vanished, and the shrunken image betokens premature decline. Both heart and mind suffer more in comparison from the habit than is the case with the opposite sex. Worse than all are the pangs of conscience, and

mortification, and grief which such a vile habit engenders. This, added to physical exhaustion, becomes prophetic of the shipwreck of all the glorious attributes of womanhood. The yoke under which she habitually labors is of such a nature that the mind moves in a perpetual circle, and from which it cannot elevate itself. The whole endeavor is to mislead the eyes of others away from her true condition, and to recall the memories and imaginations which give fresh encouragement to the lascivious practice.

19. And yet another kind of moral deformity may spring up from the practice. The mind accustomed only to its own selfish broodings and lascivious thoughts, does not feel at ease in other spheres of thought. The pleasure of self-abuse then becomes the chief delight of those erring misses, and they give themselves up to it. All pleasure of concourse of the sexes is lost, and nothing but loathing and indifference takes its place. Their own silent, or rather secluded indulgence, eclipse the higher and nobler enjoyments. The sexual impulse with such is perverted and usurps dominion, and is much more frequent, according to Tissot, in women than in men. He cites the case of a wife who had become so confirmed in the habit of masturbation that she esteemed the pleasure

superior to marital intercourse, for which she felt an unmitigated disgust. Tissot also remarks that this abominable habit keeps some girls from marrying at an age when they could do so; because in their estimation, it would deprive them of this unnatural method of gratifying their passions, and hence the increased number of old maids.

20. It is true that the fluids lost by women by masturbation are less vital and perfect than that lost by men, and for this reason women can endure these exercises longer and more frequently without apparent injury. But the longer and oftener the woman gives herself up to the practice, the more serious the consequences becomes, and this is attributable to the delicate organization of the female system.

21. Among the examples of broken down constitutions, occasioned by the vice, we find recorded numerous instances of confirmed melancholy and insanity, nymphomania, idiocy and suicide. Dr. V. Graifa, of Berlin, relates a remarkable case of recovery from idiocy in a young woman after the amputation of the clitoris and the cessation of masturbation.

22. The TREATMENT required for impaired female constitutions, so long as reason and moral sense remains, must primarily be moral—onanism must be

discarded, denounced and condemned. The mind must be directed to higher aspirations and purer thoughts, and for the debility and loss of strength, a good wholesome diet, and exercise in the open air are commended, with two doses of China daily until relieved. For the cramps of the incipient stage give Nux vomica and Sepia 3d decimal, whenever they occur. For the weary, tired and listless feeling, Arnica, third decimal, may be taken twice a day. For nervousness and hysteria or for timidity and spasm, Hyoscyamus may be given three or four times during the day. If dejected and inclined to weep, Ignatia. For epileptiform troubles, Cuprum met. Loss of mind and memory, Sulphur. For nymphomania, Cantharis. All of these remedies may be employed in the 3d decimal attenuation, and prepared for administration in the usual way.

23. Certain aliments are prohibited, such as oysters, eggs and indigestible meats, and all stimulating beverages. By following the above directions all will be accomplished that can be in the way of restoring sound health.

CHAPTER X.

1. Spermatorrhœa, as before stated, consists of unconscious seminal emissions, that occur from the most trivial excitement, distinct from the disease-producing causes on which it depends. It gives rise to a series of symptoms of great importance to the entire organic structure of man. It is not only evident that the causes of spermatorrhœa sometimes remain, but that they effect pathological changes in different parts of the genital organs. The disturbances which are wholly due to the seminal losses are as follows:

2. The entire organism becomes altered and impaired; the sufferer without being able to fix the locality of the pain, and probably without realizing the nature of his trouble, is beset with general discomfort, lassitude and trembling weakness of the extremities—a depressed condition of the entire body, and a

distaste for any occupation of body or mind; not fully realizing the nature of his trouble, nor able to explain, he retires exhausted, sleeps indifferently, and awakes without having been refreshed or improved in strength, with a sense of pressure, fullness and dizziness of the head, and inclination to fainting.

3. An enfeebled and sick body is but a feeble instrument for the mind that depends upon the cerebral-center for its integrity. It must therefore suffer when the body is thus depressed. Its activity is seriously impaired and morbid. The fire of the intellect can glow but faintly when the whole physical system is in such a flickering condition. For matter and spirit are so closely and intimately related in human beings, there must be a reciprocal influence of each upon the other, or a perpetual conflict between nature and spirit, body and soul, or matter and force.

4. And to add to the misery and wretchedness, a knowledge of its source, or a self-consciousness of guilt, and the probability of having become the victim of incurable disease, only opens the channel for fearful and tormenting forebodings. Impotence is morti_ fying, and to be in this hopeless condition fills the mind with despair and leads to confirmed melancholy.

5. Then, further, a continual depression of spirits

and brooding over this unpleasant condition, leads to
intemperate stimulation, and this to affections of the
brain, and a train of evil consequences that betokens a
complete wreck of body and mind, the fruits of which
may culminate in despair and suicide, or in insanity or
idiocy, and the absolute loss of mental impressibility,
and finally a sinking away in exhaustion, or an apoplectic convulsion may end the train of evil consequences of self-abuse and spermatorrhœa.

6. There is another class of symptoms that sometimes shows itself as the consequence of abnormal
seminal losses. This class embraces great muscular
weakness and different forms of paralysis. There is
an intimate relation and mutual dependence that exists
between the nervous system and the blood; nervous
energy depends on the purity and normal condition of
the blood. An impoverished condition of the circulation explains the diminution of muscular power. For
it is self-evident that the *vis nervosa*, which is the
natural stimulant of muscular power, must cease to
be active in the degree that it fails of support from
the blood. Spermatorrhœa not only deprives the circulation of the purest elements of the blood, and thus
produces an irritable condition of the nervous system,
but by reflex irritability the nearest spinal nerves and

thence the whole cerebro-spinal system may become affected; and by continuity the muscles become subject to extreme weakness and paralysis. As for example the lower extremities sometimes exhibit a semiparalytic condition, causing the victim at every step to throw his legs irrespective of muscular control.·

7. Paralysis of the bladder, rectum and anus follow, and the muscles of the hip also become implicated. Sometimes only a single locality becomes paralyzed and this may be the tongue or perchance the spincter of the bladder or anus, and this depends upon the extent of the irritation of the nervous system.

8. When brain affections are becoming more extensive, one organ after another may show the effect in partial paralysis. When stuttering and stammering or loss of speech entirely manifest themselves, we are led to suspect some affection of the nerves immediately connected with the brain, on which the muscular apparatus depends; and it does not necessarily follow that other localities will become similarly affected.

9. But inasmuch as spermatorrhœa being in some instances, the primary cause of paralysis of the tongue, this symptom has been regarded as ominous of more serious troubles when the losses of semen are persistent. It may be the first alarm of an increasing or

progressive paralysis that may terminate in general mania, and on this account the symptoms have been studied in lunatic asylums as the prodromous or forerunner of alarming results.

10. That the most frightful cases of chorea arise from self-abuse and seminal losses, no reasonable doubt obtains. The irritation of the brain which results therefrom, causes a semi-paralytic condition of the facial muscles, which gives numerous twitchings and a peculiar expression to the face, and if not obviated there may arise a more extensive paralysis implicating the optic and auricular nerves, and those of the palpebral muscles, rendering it difficult to open or close the eyes.

11. But the effect does not end with mere weakness of sight. Rognita describes a case of amaurosis from excessive seminal losses in a young Jesuit from Palermo, who indulged in self-abuse six or seven times a day. Deslandes considers the amaurosis a symptom of great exhaustion, and of a parallel character with that of the legs from spinal irritation. In addition to this blindness, the motor muscles of the eye may become sadly affected, and strabismus and spasms of the greatest intensity may take place, and also a constant lachrymation and agglutination of the eyelids in the morning.

12. It must be confessed that spinal irritation is one of the most disagreeable consequences of spermatorrhœa. It is a diseased condition intermediate between nerve pain and inflammation, and is denoted by a pressing, drawing sensation in the region of the hips and small of the back; disturbed sensibility, formication, alternation of coldness and heat, pressure and weight, and pain in bending down, and through the enfeebled genitals the irritation extends to the lower portion of the spinal cord, and is reflected to the testes and penis, producing in them a sensation of drawing, pressure and dullness, extending to the inguinal and hypogastric regions, and from thence it may be reflected upwards to other organs, producing an uncontrollable restlessness.

13. A super sensitiveness of the entire organism is liable to result. The auricular nerves are too sensitive to endure loud talking, music and the like. The subject is unable to concentrate his thoughts on any subject. He can neither endure the act of reading or writing, and he must therefore, remain inactive, beset with sleeplessness, headache, dizziness, perverted taste and smell, and pricking and itching of the skin.

CHAPTER XI.

THE EFFECT OF SPERMATORRHŒA UPON THE RESPIRA-
TORY SYSTEM AND THE HEART AND OTHER ORGANS.

1. In the course of the general irritation of the nervous system, arising from spermatorrhœa, the breathing apparatus becomes implicated, and oppression of the chest and præcordial anxiety weigh heavily upon the patient. A short, dry, and persistent cough most always results from the sensitive condition of the pulmonary and bronchial nerves, and palpitation of the heart sets in to complete the picture. Nearly every authority upon the causes of sexual diseases allude definitely to the asthmatic symptoms produced by pollutions and spermatorrhœa; associated with these are dry cough, debility, feebleness, restlessness, perspiration and stitches, which actually imitate the symptoms that usually accompany tuberculosis. Many a practitioner has been puzzled to institute a diagnosis, to tell the difference.

2. Diseases of the heart and large blood vessels frequently result from self-abuse and spermatorrhœa, and sometimes from excessive sexual indulgence. Nevertheless, organic trouble of the heart may be present without any lesion. In such cases the appearance is due to spinal irritation alone, which extends in a greater or less degree to the medulla oblongata and cerebellum, and this also explains the unbearable pain and sensation of pressure at the nape of the neck and back of the head, and the tendency to bend backwards as in opisthotonos of the neck in transient tetanus.

3. Gouty pains in the feet and knees, or hands and fingers, in conjunction with convulsive movements and trembling are also consequent upon self-pollution and spermatorrhœa. Epilepsy and chorea frequently follow sexual excesses—the latter more frequently in young girls troubled with thread worms, who, through their biting and itching influences, have led to rubbing and masturbation.

4. Through disturbed innervation the nerves of the stomach become implicated, producing pains, cramps and spasms, and through the general deterioration of the body indigestion and defective nutrition may result. The torpor of the muscular system through-

out all the organs retards or depresses the vital activity
of all the organic functions, and loss of appetite, dys-
pepsia and depression of spirits are certain to render
mind and body uncomfortable.

5. The vitality of the skin becomes impaired and its
function interrupted, and when distended by foul gases
in the stomach, and wind, the condition fully accounts
for the severe colic and cessation of peristaltic action,
accompanied by constipation from which the victim
continually suffers. Constipation is one consequence
of spermatorrhœa, and it serves at the same time to
stimulate a renewal of seminal losses.

6. Constipation and hæmorrhoids, which frequently
exists at the same time, are probably classed among
the products of continual seminal losses, and also other
affections implicating the neck of the bladder and
prostate gland. The bladder cannot long remain in a
healthy condition under such a pressure, neither can
the urethra escape the sad effects of strictures or dila-
tation and weakness, strangury and incontinence, together with mucous or purulent discharges.

7. But one of the saddest of all consequences is the
final culmination of habitual seminal losses in complete impotence, which may be of two kinds—a total
inability for sexual intercourse, or want of power to

impregnate when the ability for coitus remains. The first kind of impotence may be physical, which depends upon a feeling of disgust and hatred on the part of a man toward his wife, or from too strong an attraction towards each other, or from a morbid imagination of the consequence of former sins, and above all the lack of self-confidence which one formerly addicted to solitary habits is prone to experience in matrimonial relations.

8. Niemeyer says, that young men engaged to be married frequently experiment on lewd women previous to their wedding day, and find that they are unable to have sexual intercourse, and on this account consider themselves impotent; and that such cases argue a lack of self-confidence, which must be cultivated on looking forward to the married state; not by lewdness and expenditure of strength with harlots, but by looking chastely on marriage as the forerunner of begetting offspring, and then his manhood is strengthened and he comes off victoriously the father of many children.

9. The second cause of impotence is natural when the power of erection is lost through diseases described in preceding chapters. Onanists acquire it by pollution and spermatorrhœa, which cause the membrum virille to retract and become flaccid and flabby. The

semen with such flows without erections and contact with the opposite sex, however tempting and voluptuous they may be, fails to stiffen the flaccid member, and the matrimonial couch affords no guarantee of a better fortune. If perchance a temporary erection occurs, and especially if artificial, a premature discharge of semen is certain to follow—alike disgusting and disappointing to the excited and expectant wife. From such imcompleteness of the marriage act, the wife suffers from unsatisfied sexual desires until the nervous system becomes shattered and she falls a victim to hysteria, or becomes the subject of morbid excitement and desire that may have a disastrous effect upon health and life, and who can measure the extent of matrimonial infidelity that supervenes upon this state of things?   Another kind of impotence is when coitus is possible without power to impregnate because the spermatozoa is wanting.   Wedded life is not so liable to be disturbed by this as in the preceding variety, and yet it is prophetic of a household without a baby unless furnished from among the foundlings.

10. Spermatorrhœa and onanism so deteriorates the seminal fluid, that it becomes watery and thin, and powerless, and all chance of fertilization is lost, by reason of the previous abuse of the reproductive organs.

When the ejaculatory ducts are irritated, diseased and relaxed, they are unable to fulfil the design of coition —the semen merely dribbles down, or must be pressed out. This is particularly the case in contraction of the seminal ducts, when the prostate gland is indurated and enlarged, and when the muscular fibres are paralyzed and unable to promote the ejaculation of the seminal fluid.

11. The prepuce may be so contracted and drawn tight around the glans as to interfere with the ejection of the semen, and thus be the cause of impotence. The too great and painful stiffness of the member render the avacuation of the seminal vesicles at first painful, and finally a spasmodic closing of the seminal ducts and degeneration of the testes, lead to absolute impotence.

12. Cases sometimes occur with strong and vigorous men, troubled with violent erections when no evacuation of semen takes place during sexual intercourse, and it is recorded of others that spasmodic contractions of the urethra have attended violent erections, sufficient to oppose the ejaculatory forces, and prevent the flow of semen during the act of copulation; such obstacles are difficult to overcome.

13. Atrophy, and cancerous induration of the testes

are most unfavorable in regard to prognosis. Sarcocele, varicocele, and hydrocele inevitably lead to impotence, because the secretion of the seminal fluid in such
cases is hindered, or sexual intercourse is both painful
and difficult. Spermatocele, which is a swollen condition of the scrotum, resulting from an accumulation
of seminal fluid in the testes, epididymis and vas de-
ferens, either through voluntary retention of semen in
copulation or through abstinence, undoubtedly followed by impotence.

14. Such are in general and in particular the causes
of impotence, and nearly all of which may be tracea-
ble directly or indirectly to some form of self-abuse,
and such are the consequences of pollutions and spermatorrhœa, as seen in the premature decline of manhood.   The picture drawn in the foregoing of the disastrous consequences of pollutions and spermatorrhœa,
although correct to a certain extent, must be viewed
more as a warning to those addicted to self-abuse, than
a source of discouragement to those unfortunately af-
flicted, and therefore in the following chapter we shall
treat of marriage in relation to sexual weakness.

CHAPTER XII.

1. When a morbid imagination has led to sexual abuse, and the whole sexual system has become impaired thereby, the victim is no sooner aroused to a sense of his condition, than a morbid and discouraging fancy begins to influence him in another direction, and he too frequently regards himself the victim of incurable disease. But this is not warranted.

2. When a young man who from some cause or influence had been initiated into solitary habits of self-abuse begins to think seriously upon the consequences, he is apt to imagine himself unfit to assume the relation of husband to a wife, and under a sense of remorse he broods over his situation until he dreads the future, and hesitates when he looks upon marriage as desirable. But there is in the main no occasion for this, and the sooner his will can triumph over these morbid forebodings the better.

3. When he comes into a state to renounce and denounce as wicked and disorderly the habit of self-pollution, he takes the first step to regain his manhood. If he suffers from sensible weakness on account of what has happened, it behooves him to employ the best remedial measures, with hopeful reliance on them for a cure. Looking forward to matrimony is as likely to benefit him as any means he can employ, provided his motives for entering into such a state are right, and he desires to become an affectionate and faithful husband. Even if some of the effects of his former indiscretion remain, the marriage relation is as likely to favor his entire recovery from them, and even more so than if he remains single.

4. In a happy married life the incitement to sexual intercourse being normal and springing from affection, has a tendency to strengthen mind and body for the purpose. The affection of such a man for his wife, who fully requites his love, has an undoubted tendency to strengthen the sexual system. We have known instances of seminal weakness so great as to excite apprehension and alarm, to entirely pass away after marriage. But in such cases much has depended upon the previous exertion of the will to fix the mind upon chaste subjects and to avoid all excesses and broodings

over the past. A young student of the university, subject to nocturnal emissions four or five times a week, found himself in a failing condition of health, and without ability to concentrate his mind upon his studies. He applied for advice, and medical treatment. He became very despondent and imagined for himself the worst of future consequences. To encourage his hopes, and direct his mind to chaste subjects, he was advised to turn his attention to the subject of marriage, and to look forward to such an event for himself; to which he replied that his indiscreet habits had ruined him and blasted his hopes in this direction. Although he had fully broken himself of masturbation, the evils entailed was what beset him, and interfered with his health and peace of mind, and he had therefore concluded to abandon his studies, and try to recover himself in some secluded way. Remedies were given him, accompanied by encouragement to rest awhile, and try the "Health Lift." He did so, and derived great benefit. After a season of rest he returned with ability to complete his studies, not cured of his infirmity, but greatly improved; after which he left the university and went into business, and soon became engaged to a lovely lady for whom he cherished the purest affection. But he hesitated and delayed entering upon marriage un-

til advised that such an event might obviate and cure
his emissions, and be the means of restoring rather
than of diminishing his sexual ability.   He finally took
courage and entered into wedlock and became a happy
husband, and in due time the father of several children,
and after was never troubled with the weakness that
had so preyed upon his mind.

5. The above is by no means a solitary example.
Marriage from pure motives, and not as a means of
gratifying lust, is ordained of heaven to be the means
of strengthening and perfecting the powers of manhood, and getting rid of many evils incident to a bach-
elor's life.   Love is not lust, and in a beautiful and
affectionate wife it brings love in return, and this love
is life, and full of power to overcome weakness and
give legitimate strength to virility.

6. But to look forward to marriage as a license to
whoredom must be corrupting to the wife, and a
source of greater weakness and suffering to both
parties.   In this instance lust takes the place of love;
and as lust has previously led to excesses and self-
abuse, to marry for the sake of affording it unlimited
indulgence is only adding fresh fuel to the fire, and the
physical and mental strength diminishes, and peace,
love and affection depart from the household.

7. We will therefore say to all young men that marriage from pure motives is honorable, and though the follies of youth may have preyed upon your health and brought on pollutions and even spermatorrhœa, you are not lost—your manhood is not gone—provided you exercise the power of will to break off all lewd habits which a morbid imagination begets, and turn your attention to true love and marriage; for love, requited and pure, is the fulfilling of the law of marriage; it can never lead to sexual excesses, but by the employment of judicious measures in connection therewith, it may give fresh life to the mental and physical powers, obviate disease, and cure seminal weaknesses. In order there is beauty and strength—in disorder there is confusion and weakness.

CHAPTER XIII.

RECAPITULATION AND TREATMENT OF SEXUAL WEAKNESSES.

1. In the foregoing chapters we have enumerated the causes that operate to produce the premature decline of manhood, and the numerous effects that proceed from these causes. We have also given some general therapeutic hints concerning remedies. In this chapter we shall conclude the work by a brief recapitulation and special treatment with diet, regimen and remedies.

2. In all cases the cause, whatever it may be, must be removed if possible before the effect can cease, and causes are of two kinds, viz.: primary and secondary,

PRIMARY CAUSES are those which primarily act upon the general health, inducing functional or organic derangement.

SECONDARY CAUSES are the conditions that immediately influence, aggravate or induce diseases of the seminal vessels.

3. Among the primary causes of masturbation with the young of both sexes, we have seen that worms and eruptive difficulties, that occasion much itching and consequent rubbing and scratching, are to be included; and it is incumbent on parents to be exceedingly particular with their children at this tender age, in order to guard against such initiative influences.

TREATMENT.—For thread worms, Sulphur, Santonin and Terebinth, have each proved successful in removing them. The Sulphur may be given in the 6th dilution, a dose every twenty-four hours. Should this fail, follow with Santonin 3d, morning and evening, or with Sulphur and Terebinth, in drop doses in a spoonful of water, and the Santonin in powder. This treatment will often suffice to arrest the effects of those annoying parasites. To cure the eruptive difficulty and relieve the itching, Petroleum 6th in drop doses three times a day will be found useful, or else Calcarea, Conium and Sulphur.

When girls at a tender age have been initiated into masturbation by such annoyances, serious consequences have arisen. We have recently seen a sad case of chorea which resulted from these insignificant parasites, first initiating the habit of rubbing and then of masturbation. She was cured of the malady by Terebinth 6th. She was past nine years of age, and after becoming relieved of the thread worms, her general health and strength was greatly improved. Other cases have been cured by Sulphur given persistently every night for a month. Santonin after Sulphur will generally exert a healthy influence upon the mucous membrane, and entirely obviate the itching, and therefore one of the primary causes that initiates into the habit of self-abuse becomes removed. Itching from some eruptive disease on the integuments of the genital organs, is another primary cause of self-abuse and sexual weakness. This eruption has been cured by Petroleum, and the itching entirely subdued. Conium mac. has been successfully employed for the same purpose, and so has Sulphur. The two former, when required, may be given in the 3d dilution three times a day, and the latter when required may be given in the tincture every twenty-four hours.

WHEN SEXUAL WEAKNESS is primarily caused by masturbation, there is little hope of cure until the mind, the thoughts, motives and sentiments become set against the habit, nor until the mind becomes elevated above that condition which a morbid imagination engenders. To come into this state requires a strong will, and in youth, the kindest encouragement from friends.

If, as a result of self-abuse, there occur nocturnal emissions, causing a sense of debility and dullness, China 3d dilution may be administered three times a day before each meal, or until the sense of debility is removed, or Plantago major 3d dilution may be given in the same way. Where there is a feeling of malaise and confusion after excessive emissions Phosphoric acid dissolved in water, the 3d decimal in 5 drop doses may be given morning and evening until the malaise and confusion are better. Selenium 3 may be given instead if there is vertigo on rising in the morning, or there has been an oozing out of semen when asleep, or a discharge of prostatic fluid. Sepia 6th to the 3d will cure excessive nocturnal emissions when they are followed by hypochondria, weak memory, sadness, depression of spirits, dullness of the head, and weakness of the sexual organs. When constipation aggravates the discharges, or excites them Nux vom. 3d or 6th may be given to overcome the difficulty. Dr. W. H. Burt cured several cases of spermatorrhœa, attended with much nervous irritability, with half grain doses of Bromide of Potassium, repeated every six hours for several days. Cannabis sativa has been prescribed

successfully when urethral inflammation has excited
seminal emissions. Dr. Baehr says, Digitaline will
cure the severest cases of involuntary seminal discharges, especially when there is great weakness and
palpitation of the heart.

Other writers maintain that after all the voluntary
causes have been removed, the involuntary effects that
remain must be treated in accordance with the prominent symptoms, as in case of anæmia and debility and
frequent pollutions, Ferrum pyrophosp. and China, or
in case of constipation and hæmorrhoids Nux vomica
and Sulphur administered alternately night and morning, or if strangury is a prominent symptom attendant
on pollutions, and painful erections, Cantharis 3d or
6th given three times a day before meals will generally cure SPERMATORRHŒA, which consists of an involuntary discharge of seminal fluid, when at stool
or when urinating, or at other times from the slightest
exciting causes, and especially when there are but
feeble erections, or flaccidity of the penis; and when
there is great weakness of the back and spine Conium
maculatum may be given in the 6th decimal dilution
three times a day before meals; Calcis hypoph. is also
a remedy much esteemed. A small powder of the
second decimal three times a day after meals has done
well in many cases.

Hypophosphite of Zinc deserves a careful study. Oxalate of Cerium is a valuable remedy for spermatorrhœa as borne out by clinical experience. A small powder of the 2d decimal may be given three times a day.

Ustilago madis in the hands of Dr. W. H. Burt, cured a case of nocturnal emissions of long standing when other remedies had failed.

Cypripedium pubescens. Dr. E. M. Hale administered this remedy in a case of great nervous prostration and depression of spirits, and it seemed to impart new tone and vigor to the nervous system.

The remedies in general for spermatorrhœa include those prescribed for nocturnal emissions, as well as those known to act on the spinal centre, the most prominent of which are Conium mac., Digitaline, Ferrum pyro., Nux vom., Plantago major, Selenium, and when there are great weakness, emaciation, dullness and depression, China, Phosphoric acid, Sepia and Sulphur.

While taking remedies, great care is required to avoid all medicinal articles of diet, all distilled and fermented liquors. The doses of the liquors where not mentioned are from 1 to 5 drops in water, to be repeated from one to four times in 24 hours.

By carefully studying the therapeutic hints given in the preceding pages, and making a practical application of the remedies pointed out, we confidently assert that no one need despair of deriving the most desirable benefits.

And, further, a confiding trust in Providence and a firm reliance upon the best appointed means will invigorate the whole system, dissipate fears, depression of spirits and physical weakness, restore happiness, and promote a certain return to manhood.

CHAPTER XIV.

THE APPLICATION OF ELECTRICITY IN THE TREATMENT OF SEMINAL WEAKNESS.

The effect of electricity upon the nervous system has received greater or less attention for several years. Of late it has been classed among the most effective remedial agents, and is applicable to those conditions which are dependent upon spinal irritation, and particularly upon atrophy of the cord. It is undoubtedly a useful remedy for torpid states of the nerves that convey the vis nervosa to certain parts, and as such it may be employed in the treatment of seminal weakness. But it is an unsuitable agent to be tampered with, and none but careful hands should undertake to administer it—and then according to explicit directions.

The Electric Battery, which is an excellent apparatus for treating a variety of nervous difficulties, is not so desirable in the treatment of spermatorrhœa. The interrupted currents sometimes cause a succession of slight shocks, which, instead of increasing the vital activity of the seminal vesicles, act disastrously upon them. It is, therefore, important to have a suitable electrical apparatus, of light construction, that can be called into requisition when needed. The Voltaic, or Galvanic apparatus, is by far the most preferable for effective purposes. But in order to promote its usefulness in these distressing maladies, it must be borne in mind that even the imponderable agents are powerless unless brought into certain relations in subserviency to the laws and conditions that govern them.

Therefore, in ' the treatment of these troubles, patients must deliberately, and with determination, abandon all exciting causes, avoid excesses in eating and drinking, and be always particular to shun couches of down or feathers, because the toleration of these might interfere with the use of the battery. It is also incumbent on patients to avoid all violent exercise or excessive physical exertion, and to keep the mind directed to cheerful and interesting topics—to keep good, social, and improving society, and to indulge in reading useful, improving, and entertaining books.

Dr. T. C. Duncan, whose experience with electricity guides him, writes: "Electricity is a valuable agent as you affirm, and also a harmful one when improperly applied, as for example, in spermatorrhœa when it has assumed a chronic form. A strong Faradic current produces dangerous results. In cases of muscular debility, however, manifest by lameness and soreness of the muscles with rheumatic pains here and there, attended with constipation and scanty urine, here the interrupted current applied through the arms or legs, or passed rapidly over the whole body is followed by good results. In spinal irritation, anæmia or atrophy of the cord, the Galvanic current should be applied so as to directly nourish the cord from periphery to center. Both the spinal nerves and the sympathetic should be brought under its influence.

"In spinal irritation with hyperæmia of any portion of the cord, but especially of sacral or cervical portion manifest by eneuris, nocturnal erections and emissions and vertigo, attended with lethargy and vertigo, in such conditions, then the Galvanic current should be so directed as to relieve the spine, and at the same time, nourish the organs in front. One of the most convenient for treatment of these cases is the McIntosh combined twelve cell Electric Battery. When or-

ganic stricture, however slight, continues the irritation that gives rise to spermatorrhœa, a mild Galvanic current is a speedy and very efficient agent, used
in conjunction with other means already recommended
by you."

CHAPTER XV.

When from self-abuse, whether from hæmorrhoids, pin-worms or any other cause, the victim becomes restless and feverish. *Aconite* 3d dilution may be given, and repeated once in three hours until the feverish symptoms pass away.

When the genitals become excited from hæmorrhoids, and the patient suffers from nightly erections and emissions, *Æsculus glabra* and *Æsculus hippocast.* in the 3d dilution, five-drop doses three times a day. When ascarides or any eruption have been the cause of indicating self-abuse in young boys or girls, *Ammonia* in the 1st dilution may be used advantageously as a lotion to allay the itching and thus to arrest a pernicious caper.

In case of complete prostration and impotence, testes cold, swollen, hard, painful, pollutions from irritable weakness with the passage of prostatic juice during a hard stool—a general loss of vitality from self-abuse, with melancholy, mental destruction, self-contempt, general debility and spermatorrhœa, *Agnus castus* in the 3d or 6th dilution may be given in five-drop doses in water three or four times a day.

If there is great depression of spirits, with suicidal proclivities, after prostration from onanism and nocturnal emissions, *Aurum muriaticum* in the 3d or 6th trituration given in two-grain doses morning and evening will have a good affect.

It sometimes happens that shocks, mechanical injuries, bruises and spinal injuries are followed by seminal weakness and spermatorrhœa and from the general condition of the system, *Arnica* is the most appropriate remedy. Drop doses of the 2d dilution may be repeated every two hours.

In case of sexual excess, resulting in seminal emissions attended with reeling and confusion of the head, Bovista 3d centesimal trituration in two-grain doses, repeated every hour.

Against a disposition to onanism, *Calcarea* is an important remedy. It is also a good remedy for nocturnal emissions.

For frequent nocturnal emissions, spermatorrhœa from relaxed penis early in the morning in bed without sensative discharge of blood or semen mixed with blood, with excessive desire for sexual intercourse, and at times, satyriasis, or nymphomania. *Cantharis* 3d dilution is indicated in drop doses, frequently administered.

Carbo vegetabilis for unconscious self-pollutions during sleep, or for self-pollutions without any sensation may be given in the 3d trituration, in daily doses at night.

For impotence with lacivious fancies, and nightly involuntary emissions, excessive debility from seminal losses and for onanism and its effects, China is an excellent remedy. It may be given in drop doses of the tincture, or in the 2d trituration, two grains repeated every three hours.

Cocculus is indicated for seminal emissions at night when there is great excitement of sexual desire, and drawing sore pain in the testes when touched, 3d decimal, five-drop doses in water three times a day.

Conium mac. for pollutions, with more or less pain in the back, painful seminal emissions, sexual desire without erections.

Cuprum met. cured a case of epilepsy brought on by self-abuse when other remedies failed, three-grain doses were given daily for more than two weeks. [Cypripedium, says Dr. E. M. Hale, cures spermatorrhœa, attended with great nervous prostration and depression of spirits.]

Digitalis and Digitaline are indicated for spermatorrhœa attended with violent beating of the heart on slightest motion, irritation of the sexual organs with painful erections night and day—pollutions always accompanied by lewd dreams and subsequent pains in the penis.   Dr. Baehr says: " Digitaline will cure the severest cases of involuntary seminal emissions when there is great weakness and palpitation, 3d trituration, two grain powder, three times a day.

Eryngium aquat. may be employed against profusion, nightly emissions with erections. Semen passes by day with the urine, lassitude and depression, decrease of virile power, and dull, dragging pain in lumbar region.

Ferrum hypophosphite for pale, sickly females who suffer from masturbation, 3d trituration, three grain powder morning and evening.

Gelsemium for spermatorrhœa from relaxation and debility, involuntary emissions of semen without erections, seminal weakness of the seminal vesicles, emission of semen during stool, relaxed and cold genitals, nocturnal emissions with lewd dreams, followed by quiet languor and irritability of mind.

In both sexes, suffering from excessive lascivous desire and exposure of the pudenda, *Hyoscyamus* will give relief.

Iris versicolor, for spermatorrhœa with pale face, sunken eyes depression of spirits, confusion of mind depressed, and nocturnal emissions with amorous dreams. In all cases where the dilution and dose are not mentioned the 3d may be employed in five drop doses in pure water, repeated three or four times a day.

Kali brom. in the 3d trituration may be given three times a day, in three-grain powders, to cure nocturnal emissions with amorous dreams and erections.

In cases of onanism with epilepsy and nocturnal emissions with a thrill of delight and profuse night sweats, *Lachesis* is an excellent remedy given every three hours in five-drop doses of the 6th and 30th dilutions. Cuprum may be associated with this remedy for female epileptics from masturbation, especially when the suffering is nocturnal.

Lycopodium is indicated when there is great mental, nervous and bodily weakness, constipation of the bowels, cold, relaxed and flaccid penis, feeble erections, falls asleep during an embrace, the result of excessive and exhausting pollutions. The 6th dilution ten drops in a third of a tumbler of water may be given in dessert spoonful doses, every three hours. Mercurius is indicated when there is lascivious excitement and painful nightly emissions, the sperm mixed with blood, bowels constipated. Nux vom. also is indicated for involuntary emissions during sleep when there is constipation and the penis becomes relaxed during an embrace. From the 3d to the 30th trituration of these remedies may be employed in three-grain doses every night before retiring.

For nightly erections and amorous dreams and emissions after waking, *Opium* in the 3d dilution or 3d trituration may be given twice daily until a change.

One of the best and most effectual remedies for loss of sexual desire, with alternations of erections and sudden relaxation of penis preventing emissions, or onanism when the patient is distressed and the victim of hypochondriasis, by the culpability of his indulgence is *Phosphoric acid* 3d aqueous dilution in five-drop doses, repeated at intervals of three hours during each day, until a change.

Petroleum when the habit is brought on by an itching eruption on the integuments of the testes, and from rubbing or scratching, has cured both the itching and the pernicious habit, 3d dilution in three-drop doses three times a day.

Platina is an effectual remedy of satyriasis and excessive sexual desire in the male and for nymphomania in the female, 6th trituration daily doses of three-grains. In both sexes *Pulsatilla* can be employed in obviating deranged conditions of the sexual organs. In the case of men affected with desire almost amounting to priapism. And in women who suffer from headache, backache and weariness after self-abuse, or sexual excesses. And also when men experience emissions after onanism.

When spinal irritation results from onanism or sexual excesses, and the pain in the back is of a tearing or contusive nature, worse when at rest, and the patient suffers from increased sexual desire and nocturnal emissions. The 2d or 3d dilution of *Rhus tox.* taken in drop doses in a dessert spoonful of water and repeated every three hours will afford great relief.

Sabadilla will cure nymphomania from ascarides. *Selenium* seminal emissions followed by lameness or Staphisagria may be employed in cases of long standing masturbation with hypochondriasis and constant uneasiness, fearfully troubled with imaginary disease, 3d dilution, five-drop doses three times a day.

Self-abuse caused by ascarides which provoke the patient to rub and scratch, and unconsciously inaugurate a bad habit and consequent nocturnal emissions has been cured by *Sulphur*, Sepia and Terebinth, that is, the cause has been removed by these remedies as well as the inclination to self-abuse and the consequences.

In cases of nervous exhaustion and restlessness with fancies. The Hypophosphites of lime and soda in three-grain doses in a little syrup), repeated before each meal have had a quieting and strengthening effect.

An epicurean diet of game, shell-fish seasoned with salad dressings and sauces, should be avoided.

A CATALOGUE OF BOOKS

PUBLISHED BY

DUNCAN BROTHERS.

The books in the following list are of special interest, considering, as they do, nearly all the diseases of humanity and their Homœopathic treatment. These works may be obtained of any bookseller, or will be sent by mail, on receipt of the printed prices, postpaid, to any address in the United States, Canada, Europe, the Orient, or the Isles of the Sea. No risks are assumed, either on money or books.

Descriptive Catalogues furnished free on application.

DUNCAN BROS.

133 and 135 Wabash Ave., Chicago.

A Hand-Book on the Diseases of the Heart, and their Homœopathic Treatment. By W. P. Armstrong, M. D., formerly Lecturer on Diseases of the Heart; Member of the American Institute of Homœopathy, etc. One volume, 240 pages. Cloth bound, $1.50.

The heart is one of the vital organs. It is the great hydraulic engine of the body. When it fails all the machinery stops. A knowlege of its disorders, and the ability to cure its curable diseases should be possessed by every physician. To be able to diagnosticate correctly every case of heart disease or supposed heart disease, is what this work teaches. It is written in a plain, practical manner, and is especially clear just where help is needed.

A Treatise on Ovarian Therapeutics. By W. Eggert, M. D.

The object of this work is to show the power of Homœopathic remedies in curing ovarian diseases, tumors, etc. Price 25c.

A Guide to Post Mortem Examinations. By A. R. Thomas, M. D., Professor of Anatomy in Hahnemann Medical College, of Philadelphia. In one handsome volume of 337 pages. Cloth $2.00.

This is a work that should be in the possession of every student and every practitioner.

The directions for opening each grand division of the body are clear and thorough, and could have been written only by one who had been there himself. Chapters IV. and V. are alone worth the price of the book.—*Am. Hom. Observer.*

We are glad to know that Prof. Thomas has consented to place in the hands of the profession so valuable an aid in post mortem examinations. Not only do we learn how to perform the operation skilfully but the morbid anatomy of the part is plainly set forth. This work should be placed in the hands of our students, and made a part of the curriculu n of our schools. It is well systematized, compact and beautifully printed.—*Med. Advance.*

A New Similia. First Principles of Homœopathic Therapeutics. By A. W. Woodward, M. D., Professor of Materia Medica and Therapeutics, Chicago Homœopathic Medical College.

This is a unique presentation of the study of remedies and their therapeutic application. The selection is based upon the similar *order of succession* of symptoms—a new similia. Physicians read this brochure with profit. Price, 25 cents.

A Treatise on the Decline of Manhood. By A. E. Small, M. D., President of Hahnemann Medical College. In one volume. Cloth, $1.

Sexual Neurosis would have been a good title for this book, for it deals with innervating troubles, such as spermatorrhœa and masturbation in both sexes, and sexual weaknesses ; but the author has chosen the caption used by the quack to frighten and bleed his victims. This little book gives to the profession and the poor sufferers some practical suggestions and advice. It is essentially a treatise on the various causes that induce the premature decline of manhood and the most judicious means of removing them and curing their effects. The wise, fatherly counsels of the venerable author especially adapts it to be put into the hands of erring and despondent young men. The work abounds in practical hints for the medical adviser.

A Treatise on Diphtheria. By A. McNiel, M. D. Member of the American Institute of Homœopathy, etc. A neat compact volume of 145 pages. Cloth, $1.00.

This is a prize essay and a valuable reference book.

"The latest and best work published on the subject from a Homœopathic standpoint."—*The Homœopathic Courier.*

Abridged Therapeutics : Founded upon Histology and Cellular Pathology. New Treatment of Disease by the Inorganic Tissue Cell-Salts, the Natural Constituents of the Human Body. With an Appendix, "Special Indications for the Application of the Inorganic Tissue-Formers." By Dr. W. H. Schussler.

Authorized Translation. Cloth, neatly bound, $1.00.

Surgical Principles and Minor Surgery. By J. G. Gilchrist, M. D., Formerly Lecturer on Surgery, Medical Department, Michigan University. One volume of 205 pages. Cloth $1.25.

This work is adopted as a text-book on Minor Surgery in the leading medical colleges.

It is written in a plain unassuming style, so that he who reads may understand.—*North Am. Journal of Hom.*

Dr. Gilchrist seems to possess a rare union of surgical dexterity and medical skill, and hence we have all the greater pleasure in commending this excellent work as a sound Minor Surgery.—*Homœopathic World.*

The present volume is a very excellent work, and leaves out many topics usually discussed in books on minor surgery, confining itself to bandaging, dressing, splints, catheterism, etc. Everything is concise and practical. Dr. Gilchrist is a very pleasant writer, and has a knack of putting things very neatly.—*New Eng. Med. Gazette.*

This work is intended as an aid to students, and as a complete and convenient resource to the busy practitioner who has but occasional need for surgical knowledge. The application of splints and bandages is well illustrated by means of white linear drawings on a black ground. We commend the book as eminently useful.—*Hah. Monthly.*

A Hand-Book of Diet in Disease. By C. Gatchell. M. D. Formerly Professor of Practice, Homœopathic Department, Michigan University. Clinical Lecturer in Cook County Hospital. Second edition *now ready*. One compact volume. Cloth, $1.00.

"This work is plain, practical and valuable. It is really a guide on diet, and one the profession will find reliable and correct."— *U. S. Medical Investigator.*

I consider your work on "Diet in Disease" to be the most practical, and therefore the most useful work on the subject with which I am acquainted. No physician should be without it; every mother should have it. It is in use in many of the households in which I practice.—C. C. OLMSTEAD, M. D., *President of the Wisconsin State Homœopathic Medical Society.*

The Ophthalmoscope; Its Theory and Practical Uses. By C. H. Vilas, M. A., M. D., Professor of Diseases of the Eye and Ear in the Hahnemann Medical College, and Clinical Professor of Eye and Ear Diseases in the Hahnemann Hospital. *Just issued.* Cloth, $1.00.

This practical treatise fills a most important field.

We take pleasure in commending this manual on the Principles and Practice of Ophthalmoscopy. The work is a very good one, and will be a great aid to the beginner in studying the subject.—*Physicians' and Surgeons' Investigator.*

The treatise now before us is calculated to do just what it indicates; it tells us what the Ophthalmoscope is, *how* to use it, and what use to make of it. It is a most interesting work, written by one who is master of the subject under discussion, and who has the ability to make himself well understood; the volume is profusely illustrated, printed on good paper, and should have rapid sale. We can heartily recommend it—*Med. Counselor.*

How to See with the Microscope. By J. Edwards Smith, M. D., Professor of Histology and Microscopy. In one elegant volume of 410 pages. Cloth, $2.00.

This work is an invaluable one, and is up to date on this most important department.

The hints he gives are really useful—more than that, they are highly instructive. Every word proves the great experience of the writer, and the pleasant agreeable style of his language makes the book a fascinating lecture. And that is just a point which deserves great praise, for we acknowledge never to have read a book so full of teaching, written in such an amiable style, such as this one; certainly not in the line of books on microscopy.—*North American Journal of Homœopathy.*

An Illustrated Repertory of Pains in Chest, Sides and Back; their direction and character confirmed by clinical cases, By R. R. Gregg, M. L. In one octavo volume. Third edition. Cloth, $1.00.

Gregg's "Illustrated Repertory" is an old and valued friend, and in many a disputed case the arrow's point divided our choice of the remedy.—*N. A. Journal of Hom.*

The idea of helping our sadly overladen memories with the aid of pictorial symptomatology is very laudable . . . . This book teaches us one very useful lesson, which our careful author has evidently learned well, viz., the very great importance of noting the *directions* of pains.—*Homœopathic World.*

A Treatise on Typhoid Fever and its Homœopathic Treatment. By M. Panelli, M. D. Translated by G. E. Shipman, M. D., with copious additions including a chapter on symptomatic indications for remedies by C. Hering, M. D. One volume of 300 pages. Cloth bound. $2.00.

Typhoid fever is an insiduous and treacherous disease, and even the oldest and most experienced physician is often glad of practical suggestions as to varieties, complications and management. This work, including the observations of both European and American writers, is at once a most systematic and practical treatise, and without a peer in medical literature.

Spectacles, and How to Choose Them. By C. H. Vilas, M. D., Professor of Diseases of the Eye and Ear, Hahnemann Medical College. One neat illustrated volume. 172 pages. Bound in Cloth, $1.00.

It tells everything which an intelligent layman or even an ordinary practitioner need know about the anomalies of vision and their correction. It would, we should think, be especially valuable to opticians in towns where no oculist is resident; and if we know of any such, we could hardly do them a greater service than by bringing it to their knowledge.—*British Journal of Homœopathy.*

A very interesting and instructive book, not only for the general practitioner, for whom it is especially designed, but also for laymen, technicalties and obscure terms being avoided. Its aim is to prevent the too common haphazard and often injurious custom of choosing one's own spectacles, or trusting to unprincipled or ignorant venders. The dollar for it will be well spent.—*New England Medical Gazette.*

Helps to Hear. By James A. Campbell, M. D., Professor of Diseases of the Eye and Ear, Homœopathic Medical College of Missouri. A neat volume in cloth. Price, 75c.

This work will prove a godsend to many a poor soul shut away from the voice of humanity. The whole list of instruments designed to help the hearing are carefully reviewed.

Diseases of the Pancreas. By Professors A. R. Thomas, J. C. Morgan, A. Korndœrfer, and E. A. Farrington, Hahnemann Medical College of Philadelphia. Cloth bound, 50 cents. *Just out.*

This is a compact treatise on the Diseases of the Pancreas and their Homœopathic Therapeutics by a quartet of able men. Every physician not thoroughly informed on pancreatic diseases should get a copy at once.

Diseases of the Brain and Nervous System. By J. Martine Kershaw, M. D., Professor of Brain, Spinal and Nervous Diseases in the Homœopathic Medical College of Missouri. Eight parts. Price per part, 50 cts.

Parts I and II of this valuable work are now ready. Each part is complete in itself. Part I treats of Facial Neuralgia; Cervico-brachial Neuralgia; Dorso-intercostal Neuralgia; Angina pectoris; Gastralgia; Mastodynia; Neuralgia of the Ovary, Uterus, Testicle, Urethra, Bladder, Kidney and Diaphragm. Part II treats Spinal Irritation; Chorea; Labio-laryngeal Paralysis; Facial Paralysis Writer's Spasm.

A Hand-Book of Homœopathic Practice. By George M. Ockford, M. D., Member of the American Institute of Homœopathy, etc. *Just out.* Price, free by mail, $2.50.

This work has already been accorded a hearty welcome by the Profession.

It is excellent I have recommended it to our students.—H. F. Biggar, Cleveland Hospital Medical College.

Dr. Ockford has given in his hand-book as good a condensation of treatment as any one can give.—Homœopathic Physician.

The Treatment of Uterine Displacements. By

W. Eggert, M. D. *Second Edition.* Neatly Bound in Cloth. Price, $1.00.

Among the many diseases to which women are subject, Uterine Displacements are perhaps the most common. This work is fully illustrated, showing these displacements in their different degrees with the treatment. The book has a copious Repertory or Clinical Index, the whole making it of great value to the student and busy practitioner.

This is a neat little brochure on the above subject.—" Therapeutic Gazette."

The Repertory is excellent.—"The Chironian."

We are always glad to have one more repertory to help us out of trouble, and we intend to get it into the hands of all of our students, so that gynæcology may not mean only local treatment, but sensible Homœopathic treatment. May this volume become a household work with every gynæcologist.—"North American Journal of Homœopathy."

It clearly illustrates the different positions of the uterus when out of place, as also the most approved appliances, external and internal, with causes and indications for medicines. It will render great assistance to the physician in untying knotty cases that often come under his care.—"Physician's and Surgeon's Investigator."

We are among those of our school who in preaching and practice object decidedly to that indiscriminate craze for local examinations that characterizes so many of the profession now-a-days. We believe in eliciting the general symptoms and giving remedies a chance before insisting to know the exact nature of the local objective symptoms ; we therefore welcome Dr. Eggerts' useful book as a true guide and invaluable aid for close and accurate prescribing. Duncan Bros., the publishers, have done their part in an unexceptional manner, and altogether the book is one to be commended most heartily.—"The California Homœopath."

The second edition of this book has been rewritten, revised and new remedies and a complete clinical index added. We desire to congratulate the publishers upon their part of the work.—" The New York Medical Times."

If one wish a study of Homœopathic remedies for the cure of the lesions named, he will be able to get it in this volume. I agree with the writer that good medication is better than meddlesome gynæcology.—"The Eclectic Medical Journal."

The book is evidently written by one who has had the advantage of extensive clinical experience.—"The Chicago Medical Times."

It has many useful points both theoretically and practically. His selections of remedies are well and judiciously made; his indications are clearly, pointedly and succinctly presented.—"St. Louis Periscope."

We consider Dr. Eggert's views sound. In matters of treatment, Dr. Eggert is a safe guide, and we heartily endorse his method. The work is well printed and bound.—"The American Homœopathist."

We would gladly see Dr. Eggert's little monograph placed in the possession of all Homœopathic physicians, particularly of men who have the pluck and good sense to try all things and hold fast to that which is good.—"Medical Counselor."

Surgical Therapeutics. Surgical Diseases and their Homœopathic Treatment. By J. G. Gilchrist, M. D., Formerly
Lecturer on Surgery, Homœopathic Department, Michigan
University. Third edition. *Now ready.* One large volume
of 464 pages. Cloth $4.00.

I look upon it, *in its new edition*, as an extremely valuable book, and
exceedingly useful, not only to the Surgeon, but the general practitioner,
as well. I have read and consulted it in my practice, with much pleasure
and profit.—Chas. M. Thomas, Prof. of Surgery in Hah. Medical College.

"This is the third edition of the first work on Surgical Therapeutics in
our school, entirely rewritten and brought down to date, enriched by the
clinical and therapeutical researches of a hard student. . . . The chapters on 'Tumors,' 'Diseases of the Nerves,' and especially that on the
'Genito-Urinary Diseases' are exhaustive in their remedial indications,
and invaluable to the practitioner removed from easy access to surgical
consultation."—*Medical Advance.*

Therapeutical Materia Medica

Of 216 Remedies, by Dr. H. C. Jessen, author of
"Eczema, Its Pathology and Treatment;" A Prize Essay;
The Pathology and Treatment of Hereditary Syphilis,
etc. The most complete and concise work on the subject
yet given to the profession. Among its original and valuable features is its arrangement, enabling a rapid and true
comparison of indicated symptoms. Having purchased
this valuable work we have reduced the price to $3.50.

"This is an important work, valuable alike to the student and the busy
practitioner." J. P. DAKE, M.D.

"We predict for this book a rapid step into the favor of the students
of Materia Medica." - *The Hom. News.*

Text-Book on Diseases of Infants and Children, and their
Homœopathic Treatment. By T. C. Duncan, M. D.,
Clinical Professor of the Diseases of Children, Chicago
Homœopathic Medical College. The *third revised* edition
is now *ready.* Complete in one volume of over 1,000 pages.
Cloth $6.00; leather $7.00.

This work,—exhaustive, plain and practical,—takes up the
diseases of children in a very systematic manner. The de-
velopement of the child is first considered in its congenital
malformations and diseases. The disorders attending birth
and their management are next fully given. Then all the
diseases of the whole alimentary tract are treated with all the
fullness and precision their importance demands. Next, the

diseases of the glandular system are considered. The diseases of the child's throat, bronchi, lungs, heart, brain, skin, kidneys, etc., are very fully treated. The general diseases follow—not omitting worms. The volume closes with a full analysis of acid and alkaline children.

This third edition has been carefully revised and brought up to date, making it the most complete treatise on the diseases of children, in one volume, and a credit to Homœopathy.

The author has made such a concise compilation that his work may be adopted as a text-book of our School, and we trust that no Homœopathic physician will allow himself to be without it.—*Homœopathic Times.*

Each subject is treated exhaustively and compiled from the very best and latest literature on the subjects. Much time and labor has been expended in gathering and arranging the material for publication. The therapeutic indications are fully and admirably given having been taken from all Homœopathic sources, native and foreign.—*Hahnemann Monthly.*

Duncan's Text-book fills a long-neglected want. It is the only Homœopathic book on diseases of children written on a scientific basis. We feel glad that Duncan gives such prominence to physiological therapeutics, a branch too much neglected in many otherwise fair text-books. How and when to feed a child is at least of equal importance as to heal it, when from sheer ignorance it is made sick. As old a physician as I am, I thank Dr. Duncan for this instruction.—*N. A. Journal of Homœopathy.*

Medical and Surgical Diseases of Women, and their Homœopathic Treatment.

By R. Ludlam, M. D., Professor of Medical and Surgical Diseases of Women, Hahnemann Medical College and Hospital, Chicago. *Fifth edition. Rewritten and systematically arranged. Enlarged to 1029 octavo pages.* Cloth $6.00; leather $7.00.

"Dr. Ludlam's book includes a wide range of subjects : The functional diseases of menstruation ; of pregnancy, hysteria, etc., as well as the organic diseases of the ovaries, uterus, etc. The work is well and profusely illustrated ; its descriptions are brief and good, etc."—*The Homœopathic Physician.*

This is no mere reprint with added matter, but a complete recasting and development of the whole work. While the clinical form is (with advantage) preserved, the lectures are so arranged and multiplied that they present a systematic picture of ovario-uterine pathology and therapeutics. It is thoroughly scientific, thoroughly practical ; it is the teaching of a man who has seen and done that of which he speaks, and knows how to speak about it with clearness and elegance. It affords delightful reading and instructive reference.—*British Journal of Homœopathy.*

It is perhaps needless to remark that this edition, which practically amounts to a new Look, is incomparably the *best treatiseon gynœcology ever published.* Although this branch of medicine, having been cultivated with great assiduity, has made wonderful progress within a few years, Dr. Ludlam has not only kept fully posted in the discoveries of others, but has also himself introduced many valuable improvements. That this work should pass through five editions in ten years attests its popularity. The last contains almost four hundred more pages than the fourth, and sixty lectures instead of thirty-two. We are greatly pleased at the change in the arrangement of the lectures, which now follow each other systematically, instead of discussing certain subjects just in the order in which patients happened to come into the clinic. In short, there is no book on the subject that can more profitably be put into the hands of the Homœopathic student or physician than this. If you can afford but one book, buy this.—*New England Medical Gazette.*

Feeding and Management of Infants and Children, and the Homœopathic Treatment of their Diseases. 12 mo. pp. 426. Neatly bound in cloth, $2.00; half morocco, $2.75.

This popular elementary work by Dr. T. C. Duncan, is essentially a treatise on the Hygiene of Children. It is a valuable book for beginners, and also for physicians to supply their patrons.

Evidently Dr. Duncan is a fine baby kenner, an eminent authority on pædology and a man of no mean merit.—*Homœopathic World.*

We recommend this work especially to students and young physicians for the chapters on food and management which they will find better treated than in any other small work on this subject, indicative of the words with which the author heads his introduction : "An ounce of prevention is worth a pound of cure."—*American Homœopath.*

Diet Rules for Children of Different Ages.

These are plain, practical directions, designed for general circulation, and are abstracts from a paper read before the Illinois Homœopathic Medical Association, by Dr. T. C. Duncan, and from a public address given by him in Hershey Music Hall to a large audience of mothers of Chicago. Those who have examined these rules speak highly of them. Price 1 cent each, or ten cents per dozen copies.

Practical Guide to Homœopathy for Family and Private Use. By Drs. Pulte, Laurie, Hempel, Ruddock, Burt, Verde, and others. Paper, 25 cts; cloth, 50c.

The demand for a compact and yet plain guide for the use of Homœopathic remedies has produced this work that has had a very large sale. It is just the guide for the beginner.

The Law of Cure. By T. M. Triplett, M. D.

This is a stirring pamphlet that awakes and arouses enthusiasm of Homœopathy. Per hundred, $2.00; 200 with card printed upon them, $4.00.

The Progress of Medicine as Influenced by Homœopathy. By A. J. Clark, M. D.

This is a new tract that is destined to have a large run. Price, per 100 copies $1.00; if 200 is taken and card printed on back, $2.00; 500 copies, with card, $4.00.

How to Feed Children to Prevent Sickness. Bound in paper, 10 cts.; cloth 25 cts.

This is the substance of an address, by T. C. Duncan, M. D., delivered to a company of mothers. It bears chiefly on the avoidable causes of sickness among children.

Sun Stroke and its Homœopathic Treatment. By C. B. Knerr, M. D. Price, 15 cents.

This brochure treats a grave emergency in a plain, practical manner; coming from an associate of Father Hering, it bears the mark of scientific exactness and reliability.

The Prevention of Congenital Malformations, Defects and Diseases. By J. C. Burnett, M. D., editor *Homœopathic World* Price, 25 cents.

This little treatise suggest the possibility of a great work. If congenital malformations can be prevented it will prove a great blessing. Every mother as well as every physician should read this book.

Skin Diseases and their Homœopathic Treatment.

By JOHN R. KIPPAX, M. D., LL.B., Professor of Principles and Practice of Medicine and Medical Jurisprudence in the Chicago Homœopathic Medical College; late Clinical Lecturer and Visiting Physician to Cook County Hospital; Member of the American Institute of Homœopathy; Member of the College of Physicians and Surgeons, Ontario; Author of Lectures on Fevers, etc., etc. *Third Edition now Ready.* Price, $2.00.

What is said of this valuable work:

The Hahnemann Monthly says: "Dr. Kippax has given us in this book *excellent material* briefly disposed and well described. The *Homœopathic indications are excellent.*"

The Homœopathic Physician says: "To the busy practitioner, as well as to the student who desires to quickly gather a hint as to *the diagnosis or treatment of any skin affection* Dr. Kippax's Hand Book will be of service."

The American Homœopath says: "The book will be found a useful guide in the study *of skin affections and their treatment.* We have been in the habit of commending it to students, and find the new edition still more useful as a Hand Book."

The Medical Counsellor says: "The third edition of Kippax on Skin Diseases differs from the first published in 1880 in the revision of the text as necessitated by the advances made in dermatology during the last few years. The book is conveniently arranged, is concise, and answers well the purposes of a hand-book."

The Physicians and Surgeons Investigator says: "No matter whether a doctor is a Homœopath, or any other, he will do well to read this work. He can obtain an understanding of the *diseases of the skin more thoroughly* from this book than from almost any other. We congratulate the author and publishers on producing such *an interesting work.*"

The Chironian says: "The rapid sale of the second edition, and the demand for a third, shows conclusively that a book of this kind was needed. Dr. Kippax has compactly and conveniently arranged a large amount of material. The student or busy practitioner who desires a reliable guide in the treatment of skin diseases cannot do better than to procure a copy of this work."

Cincinnati *Eclectic Medical Journal* says: "As the diagnosis and treatment of skin diseases is a difficult matter for most physicians, they may be glad to consult a new authority (American), and see what Homœopathy promises for relief. In a brief examination of the work the author seems to describe disease as he has observed it, and where he has seen the necessity for potent means he employs them."

The North American Journal of Homœopathy says: "That the second edition is a great improvement on the first one, even a superficial glance will show; and the therapeutics of *each disease* are given more thoroughly. Alphabetically the diseases are mentioned, an easy plan, as it passes over the difficulty of dividing them scientifically. (How that word is abused), but authorities differ, and who shall be the judge?"

Analysis of Acute and Chronic Diseases and Their Supposed Causes. By C. P. Jennings, S. T. D. Price 15 cents.
The basis for acute and chronic diseases is well established in this pamphlet, and the therapeutic procedure for both well marked.

How to be Plump; or, Talks on Physiological Feeding. By T. C. Duncan, M.D., editor of *The United States Medical Investigator*, etc. Neatly bound in cloth, 25 cents.
This novel work is practical, and should be read by all.

Teething and Croup. By W. V. Drury, M.D., M.R.I.A., formerly Physician to the Children's Department, London Homœopathic Hospital. One neat little volume. Price, 25 cents.
This little work is full of practical suggestions as to the management of children suffering from teetning disorders, and that much dreaded disease croup. The notes from the American editor adds to its usefulness.

Diseases of the Rectum; Their Homœopathic and
Surgical Treatment. By M. AYERS, M.D. Price, 75c.

There is a good deal of practical information in the book.—*Buffalo Medical and Surgical Journal.*

I have read "Diseases of the Rectum" with interest and profit. We need more such painstaking and discriminating observers.
Yours truly, G. E. CLARK.

Dr. Mortimer Ayres' modest little monograph on Diseases of the Rectum is just such a work as thousands of physicians need, and we hope it may find many purchasers.—*American Homœopath.*

This is a neat work on a subject, that we feel, should be more thoroughly understood, by the general practitioner. It is the practical ideas of a practical man, we should judge, and fills a much needed want.—*The Regular Practitioner.*

Dr. Ayres' work is well written and concise, and we are glad to say most excellently bound. It treats briefly, but clearly, of the most important diseases of the rectum, and will pay perusal.—*The Chironian.*

The author of this work has endeavored to present in a convenient and condensed form as great amount as possible of practical information concerning the most common diseases of the rectum and anus.—*Chicago Medical Times.*

The author, having had great success in treating diseases of the rectum, presents to the profession in this book the results of his own experience, and adds a very good condensation of the general literature of the subject.—*American Homœopath.*

This book will prove a useful practical work to the physician and surgeon, for rectal and anal complaints are not as easily diagnosed or treated to admit of our ignoring the ripe experience of our able colleague.—*The Homœopathic World.*

A good book written in plain style and no attempt made to mystify the plain reading by scientific hypothesis. The Homœopathic treatment is reliable, perhaps too much condensed, but the cry for condensation is now fashionable. So much surgery as Ayers teaches every physician should be able to perform, and that is another recommendation.—*The North American Journal of Homœopathy.*

Surgical Emergencies and Accidents. By J. G.

Gilchrist, M.D., Professor of Surgical Pathology and Therapeutics, in the State University of Iowa; formerly Lecturer on Surgery in the Homœopathic Medical College of the University of Michigan; Member of the College of Physicians and Surgeons of Michigan; Author of Surgical Principles and Minor Surgery; also, Surgical Diseases and Their Homœopathic Therapeutics. Price, Neatly Bound in Cloth, $4.50. *Just Out.*

It gives us great pleasure to call the attention of the profession to this valuable book, which is designed to aid where aid is often most needed. Few are always ready for surgical emergencies.

Prof. Gilchrist has won his spurs and is an acknowledged authority in surgical therapeutics, and we need, therefore, do no more than just let our readers know of the appearance of this excellent work— a large, handsome volume of 582 pages of close print. — "The Homœopathic World."

The author has well adapted the work to the necessities of the profession, and its careful study will be found to be a great help, in times of emergency, to all classes of practitioners of medicine and surgery. It treats of many things not otherwise presented to the profession, in print, and is a very complete and commendable work.—"The Regular Physician."

This is a solid and substantial volume, and deserves a place in every physician's library. Prof. Gilchrist is a well-known writer and teacher, and a new work from him is always welcome. He treats of all kinds of accidents and emergencies in a most entertaining and instructive fashion. "Many little things," so important for the student to know but usually not found in text books, and lightly touched upon by college lecturers, are here explained in full. The plan of the book is well, conceived, and the style is easy and lucid.—"The Chironian."

"These little things" are really what the young practitioner often needs, but in an emergency the big thing is good common sense, for in an emergency one has not the time to consult authorities. Give me the good, old or young, country practitioner, who can set a leg without having the regulation splint, and who can stop a bleeding with his little pocket-case. Study by all means Gilchrist's good book on Emergencies, and hold what you studied firmly in your memory.—" North American Journal of Homœopathy."

I like the change from a weekly to a monthly. Had you continued as a weekly, I should have discontinued my subscription.
Very respectfully yours, F. M. CLARK.

The new monthly I consider a wise change from the weekly. I hope to continue THE INVESTIGATOR in years to come. It is a guiding star to me.
H. L. PERNEY.

The monthly is a great improvement. Fraternally, A. W. KANOUSE.

I am much pleased with THE INVESTIGATOR in its new dress.
Respectfully yours, A. L. COLE.

You show much good sense in your return to the monthly.
Yours truly, T. GILLESPIE.

The new form of the Journal is a decided improvement.
Yours truly, J. ADAMS.

I am much better pleased with the form of it than last year. I have about come to the conclusion that I cannot do without THE UNITED STATES MEDICAL INVESTIGATOR any more than I can my three meals a day, and that is the hardest thing I ever tried to do.
Yours truly, JOHN T. THATCHER.

I like the new dress of THE INVESTIGATOR very much.
Yours truly, T. S. TURNER.

I am much pleased with the recent change in your journal, am interested in those "Backaches" articles. Sincerely yours,
W. F. THATCHER.

I like the change to a monthly and think you did wisely in so doing.
Sincerely yours, C. A. WALTERS.

I am very much pleased with your monthly journal; I find it a great help and pleasure. Yours, M. P. BRADSTREET.

I am very much pleased with THE INVESTIGATOR, and think it the best of our periodicals. Very respectfully, C. M. SCHEURER.

The change to a monthly is a good one, and pleases me very much.
D. WINTER.

I am much pleased with it and hope to continue a subscriber.
I am yours truly, W. L. GRIFFIN.

THE INVESTIGATOR is an excellent journal and is certainly doing a good work. Yours respectfully, D. P. SHATTUCK.

I join in the congratulations upon the change in the form of THE INVESTIGATOR. Success to it. Very truly yours, F. H. ORME.

I am much pleased with the Journal and glean from it many practical ideas which I use to the best advantage with astonishing results.
Yours truly, A. L. COLE.

The new monthly pleases me very much. Fraternally yours,
B. H. CHENEY.

I will take your Journal as long as I live. I have all the volumes nicely bound in my library and prize it very highly.
Yours truly, W. D. GENTRY.